Many of us are unaware of the e[x]t[ent of people experi]encing domestic abuse globally[... This book is a clear] and enlightening explanation [of this, and, raising] our awareness, could be happening in our very churches and neighbourhoods. It offers sound teaching for the professional counsellor as well as the untrained, enabling us to act wisely and decisively, helping and supporting such victims. A must for every church!
Fiona Castle, author and speaker

A powerful and accessible introduction to this disturbing subject. A necessary and thoroughly biblical part of any pastor's toolkit.
Graham Miller, Chief Servant, London City Mission

Given that most of us have no idea how common domestic abuse is, nor how deeply it affects our relationships with God and other people, this book needs to be read twice, with some urgency, in every church. Read once, it will open our eyes to the scale of the problem which many in our churches are facing right now. Read a second time, it will help us to make concrete plans to take actions that honour God and bring hope and help to those who suffer acutely. Our churches, and victims within them, will find the plain-speaking text and the excellent bulleted lists to be God's wisdom. A truly brilliant book.
Dr Andrew Nicholls, Pastor of Dundonald Church and Deputy Director of Biblical Counselling UK

Concise yet comprehensive, empathic but empowering, practical and prayerful – this small volume will be a big help to those suffering from domestic abuse as well as those supporting them.
Dr Trevor Stammers, Reader in Bioethics, St Mary's University, London, and author of Love Lies Bleeding: When Intimacy Turns to Abuse

This book manages to cram in so much: compassion, experience, biblical wisdom and hope. Helen will lead you into new skills. Even more, she will introduce you to oppressed women, and you will love them more deeply. This is a book that is wise and practical without being formulaic. As a pastoral counsellor, I think about these matters almost every week, but this resource has already helped me as I've walked with domestic abuse sufferers.
Dr Edward T. Welch, counsellor and faculty member, Christian Counseling & Educational Foundation, Glenside, Pennsylvania

Walking with Domestic Abuse Sufferers

Gospel Hope for Life Issues

Walking with Domestic Abuse Sufferers

Helen Thorne

INTER-VARSITY PRESS
36 Causton Street, London SW1P 4ST, England
Email: ivp@ivpbooks.com
Website: www.ivpbooks.com

British Library Cataloguing-in-Publication Data
A catalogue record for this book is available from the British Library.

ISBN: 978-1–78359–595–2
eBook ISBN: 978-1–78359–596–9

Set in 12/15pt Chaparral
Typeset in Great Britain by CRB Associates, Potterhanworth, Lincolnshire
Printed in Great Britain by Ashford Colour Press Ltd, Gosport, Hampshire

Inter-Varsity Press publishes Christian books that are true to the Bible and that communicate the gospel, develop discipleship and strengthen the church for its mission in the world.

IVP originated within the Inter-Varsity Fellowship, now the Universities and Colleges Christian Fellowship, a student movement connecting Christian Unions in universities and colleges throughout Great Britain, and a member movement of the International Fellowship of Evangelical Students. Website: www.uccf.org.uk. That historic association is maintained, and all senior IVP staff and committee members subscribe to the UCCF Basis of Faith.

Contents

Series preface

Sometimes it's hard to know where to start.

Faced with a difficult pastoral problem, perhaps something we've never encountered before, we easily feel out of our depth. It can be tempting to retreat, avoid or delay, but when we sidestep a problem, it often becomes much, much worse.

This series of books provides gospel hope for some of the many life issues people face. They aren't intended to be definitive or comprehensive guides. They are primers – enough to help us know where to begin. We don't need to know everything about an issue before we can find our way forward; we just need a sense of the landscape. And once we have taken the first few steps, the way ahead usually begins to become clearer.

When Jesus saw the crowds, they seemed to him to be harassed and helpless, like sheep without a shepherd, and he had compassion on them. In Mark's Gospel we are told that he therefore began to teach them (Mark 6:34). In Matthew's Gospel, he urges prayer that the Lord of the harvest might send out workers into his harvest field (Matthew 9:36–38). You may have picked up this book because you know someone who is feeling harassed or helpless. You may be a pastor or a small-group leader seeking a little help in shepherding your sheep. You share, with Jesus, a sense of compassion for those who are struggling. You see people in need and you want to do something.

It's one thing to offer practical help – we are all for that – but the spiritual help Christ offers us in the gospel is always what we need most. This series of books aims to help equip Christ's people to be people of compassion. People who are wise as they bring the riches of the Scripture to bear upon the realities of life. That's the heartbeat of the biblical counselling movement, and it's at the heart of all that Biblical Counselling UK is seeking to do. Our prayer is that this series of books will help you as you seek to 'comfort those in any trouble with the comfort we ourselves receive from God' (2 Corinthians 1:4).

The Revd Dr Steve Midgley
Executive Director
Biblical Counselling UK

Acknowledgments

I am enormously grateful to the many men and women who have had the courage to share their stories of abuse with me, and allowed me the privilege of sharing their stories with you. The work that God has done in and through them over the years has been an honour to see, and the manner in which they persevere each day is an inspiring reminder of the hope the gospel brings.

I am similarly grateful to my colleagues at Biblical Counselling UK, Dundonald Church, Raynes Park and the London City Mission, without whose love, prayers and wise words this book would not have been written. Friends, social workers and police officers – your partnership in the gospel has been a delight as well!

Finally, thanks must go to the wonderful team at IVP, whose gentle motivation and careful editing have been a constant source of encouragement.

Introduction

The police are called to an incident every thirty seconds.[1] In any given year 8% of women will know its pain. One woman in England and Wales is killed every three days. A man loses his life every twenty-one. Globally, a third of women will know its scourge.[2] Domestic abuse is an all-too-common phenomenon in our twenty-first-century world.

I wish it were another way. I wish a book like this didn't need to be written. How wonderful it will be when the new heavens and the new earth arrive: when God will wipe every tear from our eyes. 'There will be no more death or mourning or crying or pain, for the old order of things has passed away' (Revelation 21:4). Until then, however, there is no escaping the reality. There is no denying the suffering around.

What is domestic abuse? According to the government, it can be defined as:

> any incident or pattern of incidents of controlling, coercive, threatening behaviour, violence or abuse between those aged 16 or over who are, or have been, intimate partners

or family members regardless of gender or sexuality. The abuse can encompass, but is not limited to:

- psychological
- physical
- sexual
- financial
- emotional.[3]

Within this definition, abuse takes many forms: a husband beating his wife, a wife punitively controlling her husband's finances, or two cohabiting adults (of any sexual orientation) manipulating or intimidating each other with threats. It encompasses adult children being verbally tormented by their ageing parents, and elderly relatives living in terror of their own offspring. Forced marriage, marital rape or the sexual abuse of a disabled adult sibling – these and other horrors take place, behind closed doors, each and every day.

Sadly, most of it goes unreported. It's estimated that only 35% of incidents come to the attention of the police, and most individuals will silently endure thirty-five episodes of pain before telling someone who can help. For many, life becomes an endless cycle of abuse endured in silence, but it's far from a private affair. If there are under-eighteens in the home, they'll be aware. Approximately 90% of abuse in family homes takes place within sight or sound of the children living under the same roof.[4] This is the horrific reality of many people in our local community.

And this is the reality inside many of our churches too.

In 2012, the Evangelical Alliance published their report, 'How's the Family?' Of those women answering the survey, 10% said they had experienced physical abuse. Of the men, 7% admitted to inflicting physical hurt.[5] A survey in 2013 conducted by *Premier Christianity* magazine in conjunction with the charity Restored revealed that 40% of respondents had experienced some form of intimidation from an intimate partner.[6] In this fallen world, Christians are not immune from the temptations or the pain of domestic abuse. It's how things are for some of my friends; it's the present reality for a range of my counselees; it's the way things have been for a few of my family; it's the legacy with which some of the people I love wrestle day by day.

The crucial question is this: how, as Christians with some pastoral responsibility, should we respond?

We can minimize the problem and assume that it couldn't happen in our congregations. We can collude with the problem, telling people to try harder not to make others angry and just stick with the relationship in the hope that things will improve. Or we can offer something far more radical, more positive and more lasting.

How wonderful to encourage our churches to be true communities of hope:

- serious about creating a culture where people share their lives in ways that mean abuse can come to light
- serious about reflecting God's hatred of abuse
- serious about speaking words of comfort, love, grace and confidence into the lives of those affected
- serious about taking action to protect the vulnerable
- serious about promoting gospel-centred transformation in the lives of those who have been hurt (and, indeed, those who do the hurting).

What follows is a taster of what it means to do just that – to be normal churches full of fallible people who make a real difference. This book doesn't try to set out everything there is to know about domestic abuse. It doesn't go into details about the roles of the police, social workers, Victim Support or GPs. It doesn't seek to make us experts in the nuances of the law. Rather, the following pages contain stories (some harrowing, some full of hope) to help us understand what abuse is like. This book provides words of orientation from Scripture to help promote change. Finally, it offers practical hints that will enable us to encourage people to live lives free from manipulation and pain.

This won't be an easy read. My heart has ached as I have typed some of these words. I've come close to tears as I've written the case studies (some direct quotes from those who have suffered; others a blending of two stories to protect the anonymity of those involved). It is, however, a book full of hope. My prayer is that, as we look together at the needs of those who hurt and the opportunities we have to serve them, we will all become better equipped to walk alongside sufferers and be active partners in facilitating change.

I hope that is your prayer too.

Section 1

LISTENING TO THE PAIN

1 Hidden realities

Taya thought she had landed on her feet. After a series
of failed relationships with out-of-work addicts, she'd
finally found the man of her dreams. He was rich, intelligent,
dynamic and clearly going places (in a very nice car!).
No more run-ins with debt collectors, no more hanging
out on street corners – she was in love with someone upright,
someone whom her parents adored. It wasn't long before
the wedding plans began and everything she had dreamt
of – right down to the horse-drawn carriage – was booked
for the special day. Life was going to be perfect, she told
herself . . . as long as she ignored the beatings and the
rape.

Do you think you could spot abuse? Would you know if one of your friends were trapped? Are you able to tell when members of your congregation are suffering? Are you confident you'd notice if one of your elders were a violent man?

I used to think I'd notice. I pride myself on being able to read people well. I aim for deep relationships with the individuals around me. I counsel those who are struggling in this way. It's taken many years and a painful dose of humility to reach this point, but at the start of this book I think you should know: I can't tell if someone is being abused. Not for sure.

Domestic abuse is hard to spot. A few who are suffering at the hands of their family may wander round with mysterious bruises that catch our eyes and raise questions in our minds, but most show few outward signs. Emotional abuse and financial control leave no obvious wounds. Sexual and physical abuse can be inflicted in ways that are hidden from the outside world. On those occasions when the breaks or bruises do begin to show, many are manipulated into staying inside or coming up with plausible excuses to explain away their injuries. It's rare for us casually to be able to spot the horrors that others are experiencing week by week.

Abusers are no easier to identify. They are often masters of disguise. Most present as upright members of society – affable, successful, personable and wise. Of course, there are some whose anger spills out in many directions, leaving them with reputations that are hard to miss, but the majority come across as entirely respectable. Their abusiveness is wholly focused on the individual or individuals at home. It doesn't trickle out into the wider community. They are popular and pleasant at work, people who on the surface seem to have the gifts to hold positions of responsibility at church, and might even have a reputation for protecting others and bringing good into their lives.

In the beginning

Those inside the relationship don't always find it easy to spot the abuse either – at least, not in the early days. At the start there may be no concrete warning signs at all. Abusers can come across as oozing with confidence and bring real certainty and structure into others' lives. At some point, though, it all changes – structure morphs into control. Things that are good to want turn into things the abusers say they 'need'. Requests for life to be a certain way become demands. Standards that once were preferences become an enforced way of life. Deviations from these patterns are no longer seen as irritations, but acts of rebellion that must be quashed.

We've always aimed for dinner at about 7 p.m. At first, it just seemed like the sensible time to pick. We both got home from work about six, and an hour was a reasonable length of time to potter and cook. It meant that we could both be free to leave the house again at 7.45 – plenty of time for us to get to church or the pub by eight.

Gradually, though, the dynamics changed. It didn't matter if I was tired or if my train was cancelled, my partner expected dinner at seven on the dot. If I was a few minutes late, I was accused of being 'lazy' – that I had ruined the evening and made it impossible to get to church in a relaxed state, ready to serve. The words hurt. I didn't really understand what was going on, but I thought that if I tried harder to meet the deadline, things would improve. I assumed he was just a bit stressed at work, and that maybe, if I could make life easier at home, it would help. The trouble is, it didn't. Train strikes, crises at work, ill health, faulty cookers all thwarted my 7 p.m. deadline.

*With each passing event, the tension ratcheted up. First
came the accusations of uselessness; next the claims that
I was deliberately trying to ruin his service at church. He
said it was his duty to 'train' me to do better – apparently,
that justified the tirade of criticism that came my way.
When I didn't 'improve', the punishments began. A slap,
a plate of food thrown at my head, my hands held over a
boiling pan, as I was told, in terrifying detail, what I
truly deserved . . .*

Little by little, abuse can escalate unchecked. Those
suffering often long for someone outside to spot their
pain, but friends and family rarely know that anything
is wrong.

Warning signs of abuse
The signs of domestic abuse can be hard to spot,
but the following may be indicators that something
is amiss:

Relational:
- Rarely shares anything personal with friends;
- Seldom goes out without being accompanied by a
  specific family member (who often speaks for them),
  or only puts on social media posts that family
  members would like;
- Usually turns down invitations to spontaneous
  activities and hardly ever invites people into their
  home;
- Justifies unacceptable behaviour in other people;
- Often has either very low or very high boundaries
  with their children.

Physical:
- Panics if they break or drop something, assuming they have committed some awful act;
- Has unexplained times away from work or church;
- Has strange injuries, or attributes injuries to something that doesn't seem entirely credible.

Spiritual:
- Has a legalistic view of God;
- Prays with hope for others but not for themselves.

Secrets and silence

When I was a child, I asked my parents why our house needed walls. (It was apparent from an early age that architecture wasn't going to be my career of choice.) Their answer was simple: to keep the bad stuff out and the good stuff in. We didn't want to let in the cold, the rain, the burglars, or indeed the neighbour's ginger cat with whom my father was permanently at war. We wanted to keep the warmth, the things we loved, safe.

In an abusive relationship, things flip. There walls are built to keep the bad stuff in and the good stuff out.

At first it's often shock that keeps people silent. Did the person you love really just treat you that way? Initially it can seem so out of character for the abuser that the one who has been hurt wants to give another chance; surely it could never happen again . . . It usually does though – it rarely subsides – and when the shock wears off, other ways of keeping the silence come into play.

Abusers are skilled manipulators and quickly create environments not just of pain, but of secrecy as well.

Through physical discomfort, barrages of criticism, constant fear and restricting sleep, they disorientate those they seek to control. It's hard to think clearly in an environment like that.

People become susceptible to the lies and distortions articulated by the abuser:

'I'm only doing this because I love you.'
'If you'd just do as you were asked, I wouldn't have
     to punish you like this.'
'You're worthless – why would anyone treat you well?'
'You'd never cope without me.'
'No one will ever believe you.'

If the lies don't work, then come the threats:

'If you leave, you'll never see the children again.'
'I'm not going to give you a penny – where can
     you go?'
'Tell anyone and I'll kill the pets.'
'Tell anyone and I'll kill you.'

With those messages swirling round in their minds, those being hurt stay silent. Hope of a better life seems to slip away.

At risk

Anyone can fall into an abusive relationship. No one is immune to its snare. Many who have had a happy childhood, secure relationships as an adult and successful careers find themselves trapped.

There are, however, factors in the past and present that can potentially make people more vulnerable.

Those wounded as children by experiencing or witnessing physical or sexual violence may feel that such behaviour is 'normal' or inevitable, and accept it more readily than those who have not been hurt in the same way. Indeed, some adults still living at home with an abusive parent may have known nothing other than abuse. Their whole life may have been a litany of beatings or sexual assault, and the fact that things could be different may not even have crossed their mind.

Those who come from cultures where physical punishment between adults or silent submission in marriage are a traditional norm may assume that abuse is simply to be endured.

Those who have frailties – the elderly, those suffering from dementia, the infirm, the severely disabled, individuals with learning difficulties – may find it harder to access help outside the home. Abusers are alert to these vulnerabilities and exploit them to the full.

Those who think that their faith, upbringing or status will keep them immune to the devastating effects of the world, the flesh and the devil are vulnerable too. Abusers love to single out the unwary.

It's important to note that there is no inevitable cause and effect. Someone who has been abused as a child is not destined to go on to be abused as an adult. Someone with physical limitations is not automatically a victim. Someone from a specific culture is not inevitably trapped in an endless cycle of pain. To articulate such things is to deny the Holy Spirit's power to work in people's hearts and bring major change in individuals and families alike. There are vulnerabilities though, and it's wise to be alert to the needs of those who are susceptible. The biblical injunction to 'defend the weak and the fatherless; uphold the cause of the poor and the oppressed' (Psalm 82:3) includes the call to be attentive to people's circumstances, alert to the fact that those who oppress may actively try to seek them out. This means that one of the most helpful things a church can do is alert people to the reality of abuse, and help them prepare to take action – for themselves or for their friends.

Raising awareness

Churches can play a pivotal role in helping people understand what domestic abuse is, acknowledging that it happens in congregations, and demonstrating that there are avenues of help.

Maybe your church can do one or more of the following?

In the building:
- Advertise details of suitable domestic abuse helplines (local or national) on noticeboards;
- Stock books on domestic violence on the church bookstall or in the library;
- Formulate a notice about domestic abuse and put a copy in the church toilets along with details of how people can access help (see Appendix B).

In the processes:
- Ensure your safeguarding policy has a thoughtful section on domestic abuse;
- Have a named person (of each gender) to whom those being abused can come for help and advice;

- Offer a training morning on domestic abuse for small group leaders and those involved in pastoral care.

In church gatherings and services:
- Acknowledge the pain and prevalence of abuse as part of a sermon illustration, marriage preparation course or Bible study;
- Make sure teens are given the chance to learn about abuse;
- Offer those who have been abused the opportunity to give their testimony;
- Pray for those who are being abused as part of a prayer meeting;
- Pray publicly for those involved in helping the abused.

2 People or objects?

A few years ago, I read the Bible one to one with a lovely teenage girl from church. I can't remember why, but we decided to work our way through the book of Amos and draw a cartoon strip of the prophecy as we went. Hours were spent penning plumb lines, bowls of fruit and even an (undoubtedly inaccurate) representation of the cows of Bashan. It wouldn't have made it to the Tate, but it emblazoned her kitchen wall for quite some time. At the end of the book, we looked back over the text. I was interested to discover what had struck her most. Her answer? God really hates it when people are treated as objects, doesn't he?

Most of us know that truth. Few, if any of us, would disagree. Listen to casual conversations though, and it's easy to find examples of people inadvertently downplaying the experiences of those who are being hurt. People can:

- stereotype abusive situations, forgetting that men get abused too;

- assume abuse always happens 'out there' in communities other than our own;
- pretend that emotional abuse isn't real abuse at all;
- excuse the behaviour of abusers, imagining that it's just a phase brought on by stress;
- imagine that the person being abused is partly to blame;
- trap people in their situations by giving the impression that family matters should stay private.

Worse still, it's possible to find examples of Christians who quietly turn a blind eye, even though they know that abuse is taking place. Such things should not surprise us. Even in Scripture, we find examples of believers giving permission for abuse to occur. How chilling to read Abram's words in Genesis 16:6. After he impregnated Hagar (his wife's slave), his wife Sarai is understandably upset. Nothing, however, justifies what follows: '"Your slave is in your hands," Abram said. "Do with her whatever you think best." Then Sarai ill-treated Hagar; so she fled from her.'

As Christians in positions of responsibility, we too can sometimes get things wrong.

People wouldn't trivialize or excuse abuse if they truly understood the depths of pain that many face alone. They wouldn't make those stereotypes if they really grasped the many and varied ways in which people can be hurt: physically, sexually, financially, psychologically, emotionally and spiritually.

Physical abuse

In the quietness of my bedroom, I tried to type up what had been going on. She had been hurting me for years, and I knew I wanted it to stop. I opened an email and began to document the abuse. I traced the scars over my body: the bumps where bones hadn't quite healed; the circles where cigarettes had been pressed deep into my thighs; the wavy purple line on my stomach left by that evening with the carving knife; the bruise on my foot where she had stamped on me yet again. I closed my eyes and tried to recall each punch, each pinch and each threat to gouge out my eyes. I remembered the night I was forced to sleep in the shed outside, and the morning she spiked my coffee with antifreeze. And then I closed my laptop tightly. It wasn't credible to think anyone would believe that a popular, petite lawyer would act like that. I can barely believe it myself, and she is my sister . . .

Physical pain is easy to inflict. Whether it's with bare hands or an object lying nearby, all of us are surrounded by potential weapons every day. Abusers aren't scared to use them, be it for an occasional slap or a relentless terror regime.

Pain can be a tool for control, for inducing fear, for inflicting revenge, for ensuring silence, and the way abusers use that tool can be calculating in the extreme. Frequently they are careful to make sure the bruises aren't in places that show, or to abuse on a Friday night so that marks will subside before the next day at work or the Monday school run. They are vigilant enough to use everyday objects, so there's no chance of them being caught with something unusual in the house, calculating enough to make the abused person clean up all the evidence of an attack. They are sufficiently measured (much of the time, at least) to make sure they don't kill – abusers need their victims alive in order to continue in their pattern of control.

Fighting back rarely works. Becoming numb is no protection. Abusers sense when someone isn't responding to a certain form of 'punishment' any more. They move on to something new, something more painful – something that sends out a clear message that the hurt is not going to stop.

At times just the threat of pain is sufficient to control the victim. After enough beatings, simply reaching for the long hoover attachment can be enough to ensure compliance. The mere act of picking up a wine bottle can induce sufficient memories of broken glass held to the throat to cause any thoughts of disagreeing with an abuser's request to be instantly dismissed.

Are there stages of abuse?
There can be a rhythm to physical abuse – a cycle that repeats itself week after week. First, the tension builds, and little by little the demands of the abuser increase. Each passing hour becomes more difficult to bear. Finally, the tipping point is reached and the abuse is meted out. Punches or burns are inflicted without mercy. After that, a moment of calm. Abusers may say they're sorry. They may even promise it won't happen again. But it usually will. And next time it may be worse.

The tension-fuelled phase often feels the worst. Waiting for the punch is frequently described as being more painful than the blow itself. That's why, at times, those who are suffering from the abuse seem to provoke

---

their abusers. But far from it being an act of defiance, it's a bid for hope. If they can choose the moment when the beating comes, at least they will have a measure of control. At least they can look forward to a few days of peace.

Sexual abuse

Sex has been used as a weapon of control for as long as anyone can remember. Sibling rape, sexual assault on an elderly relative or the molestation of a disabled adult child are horrors that are almost universally condemned. The physical and emotional pain they engender is hard to quantify.

Until recently, however, sexual abuse within marriage (or even in a cohabiting partnership) was considered virtually impossible. It was assumed that two people in a committed relationship who had, at times, engaged in consensual sex could never be guilty of rape or other forms of sexual assault. Thankfully, it is now increasingly acknowledged that sexual abuse and rape within marriage are real, and laced with genuine pain.

In this technological age, domestic abuse can spill over into the internet too. Forcing a partner or family member to generate pornographic content for the web, threatening to release explicit photos ('revenge porn') if someone doesn't comply with the abuser's every whim, or watching pornography to humiliate others are all part of an abuser's arsenal:

He wanted sex much more often than I did. At first, he used to ask and create an atmosphere conducive to the act, but after a while, he just assumed he was entitled. If I agreed, things only hurt a little, but if I tried to say 'no', I knew there would be trouble ahead. Sometimes he would just force himself in, no matter how much I was crying. At other times, he would leave me physically untouched, but instead lie in bed watching porn, making sure I knew just how much better looking the women on screen were, compared with me. He didn't respect me – he used me for his own pleasure and didn't care how much I got hurt.

In some marriages, it is the absence of sex, not its presence, that constitutes abuse. There are times in many marriages where sex is temporarily absent because of illness, exhaustion or other relational strife (or for prayer; see 1 Corinthians 7:5) – these things are not abuse – but when sex is deliberately withheld because someone is 'too ugly, too pathetic or too much of a failure', then cruelty is clearly at play.

Do our bodies really matter?

It's not hard to find people who play down what happens to the body, saying instead that it's our inner self that matters most. The soul is undoubtedly important, but God made humans to be both soul and body. He supplies for our physical needs through the provision of food and clothing. In the case of those who are in Christ, he makes our bodies a temple of the Holy Spirit (1 Corinthians 6:19), and in eternity we will have resurrection bodies with which to worship him (1 Corinthians 15:42). We are, by design, embodied souls, and what happens to our bodies matters to God.

Financial abuse

Within the home it's common for money to be shared. In some relationships, some cultures, one person will take the lead in dealing with finance, and why not? In abusive relationships, however, the control of money is firmly held by one party, with others having no real say on how it is spent. Cash becomes a method of control, a tool for isolation or a weapon of rebuke.

> *I used to get an allowance each week. It was crazy. I earned a lot of money in my job, but had no freedom to buy my own clothes. Money went into a joint account, but she cut up my card, intercepted the post when I requested a new one and demanded to see receipts. I attempted to open up once to a friend. He just laughed and told me I needed to 'man up'. As if that would help! People don't get how deep the effects of control can go.*

Emotional/psychological abuse

Emotional abuse runs parallel to every other kind of inflicted pain. Every punch, every assault, every time money is withheld, there will be the implicit or explicit statement that someone is worthless.

Words wound, and the relentless stream of insults dished out by abusers gradually takes its toll. 'Useless. Pathetic. I wish I'd never married you. You piece of dirt. Why would anyone love you?' Words in the vocabulary of an abuser paint a picture of a world that is not interested in helping and a God who is either unconcerned or complicit in the pain.

Mind games can feature too. A passport gets hidden by the abuser, but still punishment is given to the one 'careless enough to lose it'. Spouses are forced to stand naked in front of a mirror and criticize the reflection they see. At times, the abuser's words run to the extreme of accusing the abused of being abusive themselves. It is not unknown for abusers to call the police because of the abused – making them out to be the criminal in the home.

Spiritual abuse

Maybe most devastating of all is the abuse that is justified on spiritual grounds. All too common are those abusers who claim to be doing the will of God. They twist Scripture, exalt law over grace, and pretend the pain is in some way helping an individual move towards Christ.

A slap can be accompanied by an injunction to 'turn the other cheek', or a demand for compliance associated with a verse on a wife's call to 'submit'. Abusers can latch on to passages that speak of God's hatred of laziness and use that to justify retribution if their elderly mother dares to take a moment to relax. Rather than exercising the wonder of forgiveness, judgment is meted out over the slightest transgression, with the more calculating even putting into play a hierarchy of punishments, giving the false impression that each ounce of pain is measured and therefore justified in some way.

My father was a pastor. He preached every Sunday. The congregation had him on a pedestal; in their eyes he could do no wrong. At home things were very different. He used to lecture my mum on what a godly woman should be like, pointing out all the ways in which she fell short every day. He demanded that Bible verses be learned and repeated – although it was only those verses that 'proved' his point. As the head of the household, he demanded that she submit – not in a biblical way, but in an attitude of silent servitude. He told us that he would never lose his temper, but that it was right that we saw what righteous wrath was like. His punishment of choice? Beating my mum with a Bible. I resolved early on in life that I never wanted to marry a man of God.

These are the kinds of pain people endure. Some occasionally, others relentlessly. And these are the kinds of acts God abhors. As those who walk alongside sufferers, can we see just how offensive to God such attitudes and actions truly are? Will we not allow ourselves to be moved by the horrors that lie behind closed doors?

3 The hopelessness trap

People who are abused often put on a brave face. Each time they leave the house, they don a façade. But behind the mask, the effects of abuse are causing a deep erosion of their sense of self.

What does it feel like to be abused? It's emptiness. It's the absence of everything good. It's disappointment. It's like being promised a diamond and ending up with a lump of coal. It's not the bruises that do the most damage; it's the shame and the lies. The sneaking suspicion that it's all your own fault. The nagging thoughts that you deserve everything you're getting. The apparent reality that there is absolutely nothing you can do.

I used to love the 'hall of mirrors' when the local fair came to town. The roller coasters didn't appeal, but the opportunity to walk slowly past the glass and see myself morph into different shapes never failed to capture my imagination. Even with the basics of physics tentatively up my sleeve, I was entranced by the impact that the distortions of glass could have. I stayed the same of course, but my reflection constantly changed.

We all have a self-image. When we look in the bathroom mirror each morning, we see more than the freckles, the wrinkles and the bad hair. We have an opinion of ourselves that undergirds much of what we subsequently say and do.

There are some in this world who seem to derive their identity from a rose-tinted mirror. They're the people who think they're great, fine (or near enough) just the way they are.

Others of us try to see ourselves through a more biblical lens. As we look in the mirror of Scripture (and James chapter 1 describes God's Word in that way), we see ourselves as God sees us. There's beauty in every human made in the image of God, but that image has been marred by sin. For believers, there's dignity in being adopted by the King of the universe – amazingly, we're his precious, forgiven children for ever. That's coupled with the clear reminder that we're not perfect yet, and are called to change. There's pain in the world, but hope that one day both we – and the world – will be just as God designed us to be.

For those who are abused, the mirror is somewhat bleaker. The cumulative effect of the physical, sexual, financial, psychological, emotional and/or spiritual abuse pushes people to see themselves not in the light of Scripture, nor surrounded by a rose-tinted frame, but in the light of the twisted web of their abuser's actions and words. The three most common adjectives I hear as I speak with those who struggle? 'Worthless', 'helpless' and 'hopeless'.

Worthless

What other conclusion could I possibly come to? You treat
something precious with care. You're gentle with things of
value. It's the worthless stuff that you toss aside or break.
Think about it . . . If someone gave you a Montblanc pen,
you'd keep it safe in a drawer. You'd fill it with the finest ink
and use it to write letters that matter. Cheap biros? They're
the things you fling to the bottom of your bag, the pens
you chew. They're the ones you throw away once the ink
begins to fade, and it doesn't ever occur to you to mind.
They don't matter. Like me. I've been chewed out, tossed
aside and lived my life at the bottom of the pile. I'm a
disposable human being. That's how I've been treated.
That must be who I am.

It's not hard to see how it all adds up. Over the course of
months, or years, those being abused can be brainwashed
into thinking they don't matter at all. At first, they may
put up some kind of mental fight, quietly asserting
that they do have value in the home and in the world, but
after a while they often give up. It's exhausting trying to
counteract the lies that come so thick and fast. Abusers
seem so much stronger, so much more confident, than the
abused feel. It's simpler – safer – to acquiesce to their point
of view.

At times, the messages come from more than one
source. It's not unknown for family members to commit
abuse together. I still remember the first time I read a
story of a man abused not just by his wife, but by his
mother-in-law and adult children alike. All four sneered at
his 'ineptitude'; the whole family colluded in the violence.
His food was rationed; his clothes never brought true

warmth. At the height of the abuse he was forced to sleep in a rabbit hutch. They made it perfectly clear that, in their eyes, he was no more than an animal. How did they exert such power? By sending out consistent messages that he was utterly insignificant. In the end, he reasoned that 'everyone can't be wrong'.

On occasions, it gets even worse. Abusers impart the lie that the abused are not just worthless, but actually designed for pain. So low, so insignificant, that their only function is to be a punchbag or a slave. They strip the family member of all vestiges of humanity to the point of refusing to use their name. The abused become objects in the hands of those who love to control.

Helpless

People who feel they have no worth rarely have much energy for change. They start to believe there is nothing they can do to stop the abuse and, indeed, that there is nothing they should do. Such thinking is the result of manipulation, but it feels logical. After all, if you are 'getting what you deserve', you shouldn't try to avoid the punishment, should you?

On those rare occasions when sufferers do try to change their situation, they are often met with severe reprisals. The abuser exerts more control. Extended family can tell them not to rock the boat. Few have the energy to keep pursuing change in environments like that.

In time, those who are abused can sometimes believe that abuse is inevitable. They can adopt an identity that says, 'I'm worthless, I'm useless and it's right that people treat me badly, and so I'm just going to let them.'

Sometimes those who are being abused will even add to the abuse by hurting themselves. They may self-harm by hitting, cutting or burning themselves or picking their skin in order to continue the punishment they feel they deserve, or in a misguided attempt to cleanse themselves of some 'bad stuff' within.

Hopeless

It doesn't take long for thoughts that they're worthless and helpless to morph into a suspicion that their situation is hopeless. If you can't help yourself, why would you hold out any hope that others will help you? Things of value get rescued, people muse, not things of no worth.

> *Imagine your house is on fire. You've got just a few seconds to rush in and pick up what matters most. What will you grab? Some might think practically and run for their laptop, passport or credit cards. Others will be more romantic and head for a photo album or ring. Many would opt for the pets – they have a life worth living after all. There are lots of options. One thing's for sure, though, no one runs into the building to rescue the trash. Why would you? Trash doesn't matter, and you don't save what doesn't matter.*

It's the cheap biro issue again.

The psalmists expressed something of this pain. They understood human abandonment, exhaustion and hurt. Psalm 88 was penned for use within communities of faith. One counselee recently commented that it reflected well what was going on in her heart. It's worth reading it slowly and letting the depths of the despondency sink in. These are the verses she quoted to me:

> I am overwhelmed with troubles
>   and my life draws near to death.
> I am counted among those who go down to the pit;
>   I am like one without strength.
> I am set apart with the dead,
>   like the slain who lie in the grave,
> whom you remember no more,
>   who are cut off from your care.
> You have put me in the lowest pit,
>   in the darkest depths.
> Your wrath lies heavily on me;
>   you have overwhelmed me with all your waves.
> You have taken from me my closest friends
>   and have made me repulsive to them.
> I am confined and cannot escape;
>   my eyes are dim with grief.
> (verses 3–9)

For a few, the sense of hopelessness runs so deeply that thoughts of suicide appear. In the face of an unbearable life, a life devoid of love, ending it all can have great appeal.

How do I start a conversation if I suspect domestic abuse?

It's not easy for those who are being abused to approach us – often they don't feel worthy of our love, let alone our interest. So, if we have a suspicion that someone is enduring some of the horrors just described, we should

---

always start a conversation and do so in accordance with our church's safeguarding policy. This might include:

- Finding a safe place to talk (away from his or her friends);
- Saying that you are concerned about the person;
- Stating that the church takes it very seriously when people are in trouble, and that the person is welcome to come and speak about anything, confident of being believed;
- Reminding sufferers that, with God, no situation is hopeless, and no human being is worthless;
- Quoting Scriptures that remind us it is good to expose the deeds committed in darkness (Ephesians 5:11), and good to protect ourselves from harm (Proverbs 27:12);
- Telling sufferers that we are praying for them and encouraging them to pour out their heart to the Lord in prayer (or by reading a psalm with which they can identify);
- Pointing them to the church noticeboard or bookstall and encouraging them to consider getting hold of a resource that might be useful.

It is rare for an initial conversation like this to result in a disclosure (although sometimes it can), but such words often help people see that there are options, should they choose to access them.

Of course, if there are children in the home where abuse is suspected, we should follow the guidelines in our church's safeguarding policy for children as well. Witnessing domestic abuse is indeed a safeguarding matter, and if abuse is suspected, it is wise to discuss this with the church safeguarding officer and encourage this person to take counsel from a duty social worker or other professional who specializes in this field.

4 What is God like?

As a child, my love of visual distortions extended beyond fairground mirrors. Water provided equal intrigue – not just for my own reflection, but my father's as well. There's no denying it, he was a man of large ears. We joked that if he fell from a plane, he would glide. Seeing his reflection in a gentle undulating river almost blew my mind. He became positively elephantine! Some days that amused. Others it scared.

It's not just self-image that gets skewed when people face abuse; their perception of God gets twisted too. People wonder if God really is in control, if he truly cares, if he actually has the power of which the Bible speaks . . . they often doubt if grace is enough.

I sat in church every Sunday. I heard the sermons. I sang the songs. I prayed for mission around the globe. But it never felt right. It never felt true for me. I could see God's love in action in other members of the congregation. I loved to hear stories

*of how he was changing lives, but mine just kept on going the
same way. I eventually came to the conclusion: either God
wasn't as good as the Bible claimed, or I was doing something
terrible to disqualify myself from his love.*

A gentle Shepherd?

Psalm 23 is one of the best-known passages in the Bible.
It paints a picture of a good shepherd leading his sheep
with both authority and gentleness. He's a shepherd
who provides (verses 1–2), guides (verse 3) and protects
(verse 4). All those who follow him reach a place of safety,
a place of plenty (verses 5–6).

It's a wonderful psalm – one of my favourites – but one
that raises many questions in the minds of the abused.
Did God lead me into this abusive relationship? Where is
my pasture of rest? Why isn't God using his rod and staff
to comfort me? Why isn't he fighting off the 'wolf' that
tears at me day after day? Will I ever reach the destination
of victory and peace?

They're not questions of academic theology proportions,
although some will value a well-thought-through response.
They're heartfelt questions. Questions that scream, 'What's
so wrong with me that I can't see the shepherd's love and
care?' They're questions that lead people to suspect that
maybe they're not one of God's sheep after all.

A great King?

Psalm 146 speaks of God as a wonderful King. He's the one
who creates (verse 6), who rules with justice (verse 7), who

sees the pain of the vulnerable (verse 9) and is sovereign over all things (verse 10). There is no one more powerful than him, no one more committed to right. Even the rulers of this world are mere dust in comparison to his glory.

So why then does the world feel so out of control? Why is there no justice in sight for the abused? Is the pain they are enduring his sovereign will? If so, what does that say about his character? Is he just watching the abuse and sitting impassively by? Worse still, is he condoning it? Is he commanding it as an act of justice for the sins of the past?

When I hear questions like these, I'm always tempted to jump in with some good theology. Our first instinct as Christians in leadership can be to defend God from accusations like this, but it's wise for us to pause for a moment. These are not necessarily the words of heretics or of those who are pushing God away. These are the thoughts of people who are trying to make sense of the world in which they live. Before we address the theological issues, can we sense their desperation and pain?

A gracious Rescuer?

Psalm 91 reminds us that God is a saving God. He is our fortress (verse 2), our refuge (verse 9) – the one who protects because of his great love (verse 14). It's not just Psalm 91 that speaks these words. From the exodus in the Old Testament to Jesus' work on the cross in the New, Scripture has a consistent theme: God is a rescuer. He is our Saviour.

How does that fit, though, with the fact that he's not stepping in to stop the abuse? How does that square with the fact that those who are being hurt often have no place of safety to which they can run? People understand that God doesn't shelter us from every bad thing, but surely a rescuing God would give a follower a day away from pain here and there, wouldn't he? Surely these eternal truths of safety should have some glimmer of resonance with the here and now?

As for eternity, those who are being abused can find it desperately hard to believe that they would be welcome in a place of eternal rest. They've been told repeatedly that they are too bad, too useless to be able to access friendship, dignity or love. They have often had food, finance and safety withdrawn as a punishment for not being good enough. They frequently exist in a legalistic environment where unwritten rules have to be obeyed or they will face consequences. It can become almost impossible to imagine what grace could be like. It is incomprehensible that sin could ever be met with mercy. As a result, a legalistic view of God often arises – he becomes one who must be appeased, one who demands the same high standards of behaviour as the abuser and metes out the same tough judgment when they are not attained.

A good Father?

If the abuse exists within the family and has been going on for years, there are few verses more confusing than Psalm 103:13:

> As a father has compassion on his children,
>   so the LORD has compassion on those who
>   fear him.

When we look at our earthly family, we're supposed to see a little of what God is like. It's an imperfect glimpse – after all, we're imperfect people – but there are meant to be resonances between the two. For those who have been abused, this can be a complex thought. If the only 'compassion' they have ever received is the 'compassion' of a fist, then their concept of God is likely to go seriously astray.

My father abused me from the day I was born. He abused my sister and mother too. Forty years on, I'm still living at home and the abuse continues. I can't call God 'Father'. If God is anything like my father, then I want nothing to do with him. I can relate to God as my Lord. I can accept him as my brother. But he will never be my Father. Fathers are evil. Fathers can never be trusted.

How can we speak effectively into these situations in talks and sermons?

Talks and sermons are wonderful opportunities to start addressing some of these false concepts of God. A one-off topical sermon on the way God views abuse is something for every church to consider, but such an issue is unlikely to be a frequent subject on any preaching rota. Far better to be mindful of the sufferers of abuse who may be listening to the talk each week, and to drip-feed truth into their lives. We need to include phrases that will help, ones that remind us that God is not like an abusive father, but a good one, phrases that show that openness (not secrecy) in community is our call.

We also need to be mindful of common traps. It's easy to encourage married couples to bear with one another, without thinking of how that might sound to someone

who is being abused. This call flows from the letter to
the Colossians (see especially chapter 3) – and it's one
that needs to be heard – but without nuance, it can
encourage people to stay silent. We need to draw out the
difference between bearing with sin and complying with
abuse. We must distinguish between submitting in love
and being subjugated in hate.

What kind of God calls someone to submit?

One of the verses most twisted by the hands of an abuser
is Ephesians 5:22: 'Wives, submit yourselves to your own
husbands as you do to the Lord.'

Out of context, this seems like carte blanche for
husbands to make any demands they like of their wives.
It gets twisted into a weapon that wounds deeply.

That is certainly not what this verse is meant to induce!

It's meant to be an encouragement to choose to submit
in the way that Jesus chose to submit to the Father. It's
meant to be a safe, trust-fuelled response to the call to
husbands to love so very counter-culturally and sacri-
ficially that they are willing to lay down everything
(including, by inference, their desires) for the good of their
wives. It's meant to be just part of the dynamic of love that
also includes both husband and wife exhibiting gentleness, kindness, patience and keeping no record of wrongs
(1 Corinthians 13). Such godly submission can never be
achieved through force.

In abusive marriages those nuances get lost. As those
who teach – formally or informally – it's our call to make
sure that the context shines out in our words and in the
ways we model family to the wider church. It's our role to

ensure that submission is seen as a gift from a loving God that teaches us much about how he humbled himself and first served us.

As such teaching flows out of pulpits and Bible study groups, sufferers will gradually begin to see that God is stronger than the abuser. They begin to glimpse a little hope. They start to understand that what is happening to them is wrong. They toy with the idea that maybe someone in the church might be able to walk alongside them.

Responding to disclosure

It's no easy thing for the abused to speak about being hurt at home. They may be scared of not being believed or scared of being found out and having to face reprisals. The way we respond to the disclosure is of the utmost importance.

We need to:

A: Acknowledge that they have done something brave and good in opening up.
B: Believe what they have said – even if you know and love the alleged perpetrator.
C: Communicate that abuse is not the fault of the one being hurt.
D: Discern the facts. When did the abuse begin? What was the most recent incident? What has been the worst incident? Is there a risk of death? Ask (if you don't know) if there are any children involved. (It's worth bearing in mind that people may not disclose everything in one single conversation.)
E: Explore if the person is in immediate serious danger. If so, offer to contact the police, social

---

services, Victim Support or a domestic violence helpline for urgent advice. If not, ask the person how he or she would like to proceed.

F: Fix a time to meet again to discuss next steps, to pray, to look at Scripture. Ideally, include another mature Christian (of the same gender as the person being abused) in subsequent meetings.

G: Give the person a contact number for an external agency that specializes in domestic abuse and also the number of someone in church who can be contacted if the person needs to leave home quickly. (Often it is better to put numbers straight into someone's phone rather than giving out bits of paper with the words 'domestic abuse' on them – such things can easily be found by abusers.)

H: Hold a record of the meeting in a secure place and encourage the person to keep a record of any abuse suffered. Ensure that absolutely nothing of the meeting gets passed back to the abuser. Make sure that you pass a copy of your notes to the church safeguarding officer.

It's not easy to hear stories of abuse. Doing so may elicit strong emotions in us. We will need to pray not just for those hurting, but for ourselves as well. It can be useful to have a 'supervisor' or a prayer partner (outside the church) with whom anonymized stories can be shared. Such people will pray for us and help us remember that our call is to point people to their Saviour, not to become the one who rescues them ourselves (more about this in the next chapter). We can weep with them as well as pray – allow our pain to show.

Having listened well to people's stories, and having truly understood the complexity of the situations they face, we are ready to help them look to the future. And what a privilege it is to help them to see God for who he truly is, encourage them to view themselves aright and spur them on to pursuing change within the home – all by holding out God's precious words of life to them.

Section 2

SPEAKING WORDS OF
TRANSFORMATION

5 Stay or go?

I remember the first time someone told me of the domestic abuse she was suffering. A mixture of emotions swirled round my mind. Part of me was broken – the thought of my friend in such pain was simply awful. Part of me was on a mission – there was a problem that needed to be solved, and I wanted it to be sorted there and then. I don't have an alter ego, but at times I wish I did. There's a small section of my heart that yearns to be Superwoman, rescuing people from their plight. It's not an attitude that helps. It's not a stance that brings hope.

There's nothing worse than feeling like you're someone's project. It's horrible to have people who want to 'fix you' or 'rescue you'. Being on the receiving end of that just reinforces the messages that you're useless and can't do anything for yourself. I felt like a pawn in a game of chess as person after person told me what I had to do. In the end, I walked away from church and went back home. Better to be manipulated

*by someone I love than manipulated by a bunch of people
I barely knew.*

Our call is to listen to those who have disclosed the abuse and ask them what they want to happen next. Some will be in immediate, serious danger and will ask for help to leave right there and then. Others will want to take a slower approach – initially maybe wanting nothing more than a listening ear. We need to stand alongside them whichever path they take. The first route (the 'emergency exit') involves changing the physical surroundings of a person within hours, and then looking at matters of the heart in the months and years that follow. The second (the 'gentle change') takes people on a journey of hope that, we pray, will result in them having the courage to address the circumstances in which they live at some point in the future.

Route 1: Emergency exit

If someone feels there is imminent danger of serious injury or death, or simply wants to effect immediate change in extreme circumstances, it's good to encourage that person to call the police, pack a bag and go.

Please don't try to be the hero. Don't ride in and break up a fight. As church leaders and congregation members, we are not trained, equipped or appointed to restrain violent offenders. It's far better to enlist the help of the professionals and be prepared subsequently to help individuals to process what's taken place. And there will be a great deal of processing to do . . .

It can be a whirlwind experience. When leaving a battle zone at home with little more than the children and a bag of clothes, people can feel like refugees. They will need our help to focus on the immediate priorities that such situations bring with them.

We can wait for them as they file a police report, and sit with them as they speak with a solicitor about a protection order. It's a privilege to accompany them as they approach the local authority for temporary accommodation or drive them to a friend's home or a refuge near or far. It's not hard for us to provide food, replacing the essential items left behind. We can help to compile a list of people to inform – their GP and the children's school are good places to start – something that we will return to in chapter 9.

If the police are involved, they will have skilled officers on hand ready to talk people through what's going on. They will be able to refer them to Victim Support whose expertise is frequently invaluable.

We can pray too: for them and with them, reminding and assuring them of the Lord's good leading of his people, in spite of everything they are going through.

Route 2: Gentle change

Not everyone will want to move that quickly. Some will need a great deal of support before they are even ready to consider change. Many will plead with us to do absolutely nothing – terrified that, if we act, the situation will deteriorate fast.

It can be hard to be asked to do nothing. Often we can see clearly how wonderful life could be if the abuse stopped, but those in the midst of their struggles can be blind to such possibilities. Here, it is our privilege to show people a better way to walk.

How do we help them want change?

- Meet regularly (weekly or fortnightly)
- In a place of safety (probably the church)
- With a third party (a mature Christian of the same gender as the one being abused –someone who has been DBS checked[1] for work with adults)
- To speak words of hope.

Real possibilities

There were lots of reasons why I found the idea of change scary, but I think the biggest was that I couldn't quite imagine what life without abuse would be like. In some weird way, it brought a structure and certainty to my life that felt more familiar than moving away. If I broke a cup, I knew I would be slapped. If I spent too long on the phone, I knew I would face a barrage of insults about being a gossip who didn't really want to invest in my partner. I knew that if I talked about a male colleague too much, I'd be accused of having an affair. It was horrible, but it was measurable. I couldn't begin to imagine how life would be without that. What would happen if I broke something? What would happen if I chatted for an hour? What would happen if my friend Steve and I had lunch? I couldn't work it out. I couldn't risk a life like that.

One of the most important tasks, post-disclosure, is to help sufferers glimpse what life could be like free from abuse. Rather than assuming they can do this, it's important to paint a picture of what it feels like to be able to go out for a spontaneous cup of coffee, choose your own friends or say 'no' to people's requests. These little things may well be long forgotten by those who have lived under the tyranny of an abuser, and it's crucial to show that such acts are safe, desirable and fun.

On a bigger scale, it's important to describe what it's like to live with no threats, punitive rules or punishments. We can let people glimpse our families (imperfect though they may be), and when things go wrong, talk them through the fact that there will be no retribution for the burned dinner or the messy living room. None! We can even let sufferers observe how we disagree with others from time to time – let them see what grace looks like in practice.

Real options

Fact-finding is an important step too. It's all very well to dream of living in an abuse-free home, but how can that become a reality? Domestic abuse support lines and advice services are a mine of helpful information. Trawling these for details of refuges, emergency accommodation, police procedures and details of how to obtain legally binding protection orders can help bring clarity to the possibilities ahead. Knowing what benefits are available helps to show that living independently is truly viable. Why not invite a domestic violence adviser to the church and encourage those who are struggling to leave abusive situations to benefit from this person's wisdom through private meetings? Why not gather a list of local solicitors with expertise in this area? To promote safety, it's possible to come up with a code word that is easy to remember – a word that the one suffering abuse can text us, confident that we will call the police to the person's home in return.

Real perspective

Once we've helped abuse sufferers see how things could be wonderfully different, we can help them reflect on what could happen if things were allowed to stay the same. Abuse rarely dissipates. More often, sadly, it escalates. Our task, as those who walk alongside, is to be real and clear about how things might end if the abuse goes on unchecked. We don't want to sensationalize or terrorize, but we do want to ensure that those being abused understand that their lives are – potentially – at risk (even if the abuse doesn't look quite that bad right now). We want to live out the wisdom of Proverbs 19:19:

> A hot-tempered person must pay the penalty;
> rescue them, and you will have to do it again.

What does this mean for those being abused and those walking alongside? It's a good reminder that if we do nothing in the face of abuse, we are denying abusers the gift of consequences. They are doing something wrong and need to change. And they are most likely to change not if people keep quiet and hope for the best, but if the proper authorities are brought in to help them see how serious their actions have been. Bringing an abuser to account is something that can produce good in the life of the abuser as well as that of the one being hurt.

Real legacy

Those who are being abused can kid themselves that they're the only ones getting hurt. But if there are children in the home, that certainly isn't true. Children who grow up hearing or seeing abuse can struggle with significant anxiety and find it desperately hard to trust other people. Sometimes they will fall into the same traps as their parents, assuming that violence or manipulation in relationships are the norm. On other occasions, they may become so self-protective that they push others away, leaving themselves isolated and lonely, but (they tell themselves) safe at least.

It's not just children who are affected. Being mistreated affects all other relationships as well. Those who have known the pain of abuse often struggle to maintain healthy friendships – at times clinging too tightly to the people who care (desperate to taste the beauty of love), at others pushing people away (terrified of letting anyone get close enough to see the real them). In the workplace too the legacy of abuse flows on – a tendency to overwork and exert unrealistically high expectations on themselves and others, which can cause exhaustion.

At church, it's impossible to embody the Titus 2 call for older men to be role models for younger men and older women to do the same for the next generation if abuse is progressing unaddressed. That doesn't mean that those who are being abused have no gifts – far from it, many can be very active in the local church – but things at home are not just imperfect (like all homes), but flying strongly in the face of what God wants for his children. An abuser cannot be a true role model if that individual's desires lead into criminal activity. An abused person cannot be a true role model if he or she is allowing criminal activity to go unchecked, even if there are many other aspects of that person's life that appear to be overflowing with godliness.

Moving away from an abusive situation brings good not just to the abused and the abuser; it brings good to the people around them as well.

Real community

Finally, if people are to pursue real and lasting change, it's important that they know they don't have to face the journey alone. The local church is designed to be a family, one where lives are shared (1 Thessalonians 2:8) and people are spurred on (Hebrews 10:24).

Far from being a community where subjects like abuse are swept under the carpet, our churches need to be places where struggles can be spoken about. There will need to be discretion – especially in the early days if the abuser hasn't been reported and both parties attend the same church – but both the people who are hurting and those who are being hurt need to know they are surrounded by brothers and sisters who will sacrifice time and energy in order to help them through.

Should a church ever report abuse against the wishes of the one being abused?

When domestic abuse first comes to light, and the emergency exit plan is ruled out, details should be passed to the church safeguarding officer for careful consideration. The wishes of those being abused are always taken into account, but there are times when a safeguarding referral to social services or the police will have to go ahead no matter what they say.

Sometimes it is obvious that a referral needs to be made to the appropriate authorities: this is mainly when there are children in the home, but may also include times when the person being abused has limited capacity (e.g. when significant learning difficulties are at play), or when there is serious risk of death or severe physical harm (e.g. when threats have been accompanied by a lethal weapon).

Sometimes, when the physical injuries are significant, the best course of action is to take the abused to Accident and Emergency to get the wounds treated and, while there, pass on relevant information so that the medical team can discuss the option of referral.

At other times, things are not so clear. On such occasions, it is best to ask the safeguarding officer to make a call to a duty social worker (within either the local authority or an appropriate Christian organization) and seek advice. This can be done anonymously. The professionals will then be able to suggest valuable next steps.

6 Pursuing change

My grandmother enjoyed a game of cards. Having grown up in an era pre-TV, she relished the simple things of life – entertainment that didn't involve anything requiring a plug. She wasn't the kind of grandmother who simply let me win, but she did want to equip me to be able to play as well as I could. From an early age she impressed on me the importance of discernment: there are times when you need to put your cards on the table, and times when you need to play them close to your chest.

As sufferers begin to see that things could be different, they may want to start walking towards that different life. It's a journey that can progress at whatever pace the person being abused is willing to walk. It's tempting to rush ahead though. It's easy to assume the best way forward is quickly to gather everyone in the same room. In non-abusive relationships, that is often going to be the right thing to do. If there is bickering in the home, tension over shared debt, inconsistency in parenting – all these things can be resolved well by godly, guided conversation that looks carefully at what is going on in people's hearts and lives.

But in abusive situations, it's *not* right to bring the parties together at this stage.

Someone who is being abused will never feel free to talk openly and honestly about what's going on at home if the abuser is present in the room. Someone who is abusing will tend to use anything that's said in pastoral conversations as ammunition to accuse, manipulate or terrorize a partner once back home.

There may be times in the future – once all those involved have received significant individual support – when it is safe to start a conversation with everyone together, but that is likely to be a long way down the line. In the interim, it's best to keep on meeting regularly in a safe place with the one suffering abuse, and with another mature Christian, and speak words of hope.

What support can I give to the abuser?

If it's not right to meet with the person abusing and the one being abused together, does that mean we should not try anything to help the one causing pain? Absolutely not! In fact, this may well be the moment to invite the abuser to read the Bible one to one with a mature Christian. It might be the time to be more intentional about getting alongside that person in friendship. As truth comes to bear on their life, abusers may see their sin and want to admit to it. As relationships are built, they may feel comfortable asking for help to change. If abusers do own up to

---

their sin, we can encourage them to move out for a time and seek help to address the desires of their hearts and the anger within. This does not have to involve the police (although those who are truly repentant may choose to turn themselves in), but it can – often after significant periods of time – result in true and lasting change.

Pastoral and practical

What should we aim to achieve in our regular meetings? In part, it is the provision of additional information – facts that build on the general guidance sourced earlier. At times, we might take the opportunity to call in a local solicitor to flesh out more details of how protection orders work. Other weeks may be set aside for a trip to the GP to make sure medical records are up to date.

Doing this can be a bit of a pastoral gear shift, as often we can expect the medical and legal nuances of a situation to take place outside of church, outside of our meetings, but those who are being abused may not have the freedom to approach multiple providers of help. It may be necessary to make the accessing of advice as simple and time-efficient as possible.

More than anything, though, we want to be speaking words of life.

Beauty, pain and sin

We are complex beings. In all of us there are things of beauty – wonderful ways in which we love, laugh and persevere. In all of us there are scars – pain leaves its mark, and no one is immune to its snare. In all of us there is guilt – no one is without rebellion. Those who have been abused are no different. As we seek to walk alongside those who are being abused, we need to be alert to their beauty, their pain and their sin.

As we meet with those who struggle, we can encourage them by pointing out what they are doing well. Rooting such comments in Scripture can be tremendously helpful: can you see traces of Philippians 1:3–6 in their life? Then say how grateful you are for their partnership. Can you hear echoes of wisdom and knowledge within those you're meeting? Read Colossians 1:3–11 and show them how they're living that well. Or simply return to Genesis 1: in what ways are they showing a little of God's love, community and rule in their lives? You can even take non-Christians here. There is always something to affirm; no one is so abused that they completely lose all beauty.

Of course, we must also acknowledge their pain – being abused is a horrible thing! It is right that we empathize deeply with what they have been (and still are) enduring. Our God is a God of comfort, and, as his people, we are called to model comfort too. Romans 12:15 tells us to weep with those who weep, showing that being moved by the pain of abuse is an entirely biblical response. We can point to passages like 2 Corinthians 1 and remind people that the 'God of all comfort, who comforts us in all our troubles' has love and purpose to pour into the lives of those who are wounded too. Christianity is no religion of stoicism; there is tenderness for those in trouble and an invitation for 'people [to] take refuge in the shadow of [God's] wings' (Psalm 36:7).

We are called to challenge them where they are going astray too. This is the point where evangelicals sometimes come in for some flack. Is it really helpful to point out to someone who has been abused that he or she is a sinner? Hasn't such a person suffered enough? It's certainly not helpful to do that in an accusatory manner! There is never a case for looking down our noses at others and pointing out their shortcomings, and, as Romans 3:23 reminds us, 'all have sinned and fall short of the glory of God'. Similarly, there is never justification for saying that someone's actions mean that abuse is to be expected. We should never cause sufferers to feel guilty for being abused, or call them to repentance for being hurt. However, there will be rebellion in their hearts because they are human. As we saw in chapters 3 and 4, there is a place for saying that those who have been abused sometimes believe inaccurate things about God, his world and themselves. There may have been times when they have come to see their abuse as part of their identity. There is a case for pointing out that occasionally they may have responded to the abuse in ways that have been unhelpful and unwise. These things, while being completely understandable in the circumstances, need to change. Change involves turning around and doing things differently.

Most of us have a tendency to overemphasize one of these facets and underemphasize the others. Some of us may seem harsh by talking about sin more than love. Others of us will risk inducing inertia as we speak of comfort at the expense of change. By being careful to embed all three areas in every conversation, we can come close to pointing people to the love, comfort and challenge that transformation requires.

Changing clothes

The actual process of change set out in the Bible can be found in Ephesians 4:22–24:

> You were taught, with regard to your former way of life, to put off your old self, which is being corrupted by its deceitful desires; to be made new in the attitude of your minds; and to put on the new self, created to be like God in true righteousness and holiness.

Paul keeps things simple. He gives us no complex psychological models here. He simply talks about transformation being like changing our clothes.

In the midst of our pain, and in the light of our calling and the generosity of God (that he sets out in the earlier chapters of Ephesians), we should all take a look at our hearts and our behaviour. We can identify desires that are wayward. In the power of God, we can increasingly choose to address the things that are going astray. We can bring our minds under his glorious and gentle truth and, in so doing, begin to think differently about God and ourselves. As a result, we can go on to be the people that Jesus is calling us to be: more beautiful in our desires and more godly in our behaviour.

I received counselling for years and nothing changed. My counsellor poured comfort and love into my life, but always told me that what I needed most was for my abuser to change. In part, she was right. My abuser did need to change! And I did need the comfort and love that flowed from the pages of Scripture. But she left out something important. She left out the bit about me needing to change too. That kept me trapped for years. It wasn't until a pastor gently challenged me that things began to improve. Gradually, I began to realize that I viewed my abuser as more powerful than God. I began to see that I was believing my own view of myself rather than God's. I had become so used to being a victim that I didn't really have any aspiration to be anything else. I came to realize that I had to set those lies aside. I had to begin to believe what the Bible said about God, his world and me. When I started to believe what was true, I started to seek change – for myself and for the rest of my family.

Overall, gospel change is a process that can help people move from believing God is inert to seeing his sovereignty in all its glory, as their eyes are opened to the kingship of Jesus. It's a process that can help people move from believing they are worthless to seeing they are precious in God's sight, as they revel in the wonder of the cross. It's a process that can help people move from trapped to transformed as they wrestle with what it means to have a Good Shepherd who is leading them forward.

How should I pray for those being abused?

Prayer is a wonderful privilege. How amazing to be able to ask the King of the universe to bring good into people's lives! But what can we pray for those being abused?

- for the abuse to stop – and for their safety in the interim;
- for people to see God as he truly is;
- for them to see themselves in the light of the mirror of God's Word;

- that they will know what it means to run to the Father as their rock and refuge;
- that they will see the fruit of real change as they follow their Good Shepherd towards a new way of living.

How do we help that process of change progress? We point to our wonderful God.

7 Speaking of a bigger God

'How big is God?'

It's the question every three-year-old asks.

Is he bigger than my nose? Bigger than a tiger? Bigger than a bus? Bigger than the moon?

Gently and quietly, as adults, we say, 'Yes – he's much bigger than that. He's bigger and better than anyone or anything.' We have songs to back us up – many with actions thrown in.

Usually, our words satisfy a toddler. Adults are less easy to convince. They frequently believe there is no help coming from him.

The world would concur. It would have us believe that to overcome abuse we must find strength within ourselves. I remember, many years ago, attending a conference for the survivors of abuse and sitting through five minutes of a song called 'Hero'. At the end, we were all encouraged to look inside our hearts and find the hero within.

I looked. The hero wasn't there.

But God is.

As we walk alongside those who struggle in the face of abuse, whether they are Christians or not, our words need to drip with confidence in the truths that God is present and it is he whom they need most. Our job is to help them see the beauty of God's character and the difference he makes to their lives, see his unending power and grace-fuelled tenderness so they can lose their false view of him, have their minds renewed and put on truth. At times, doctrine or proposition may help, but more often, story and imagery will connect most deeply.

A bigger God in story

One of the many characters in the Old Testament who knew a bit about abuse was Joseph. As the narrative progresses, we can see him tumbling from one awful situation to the next. We taste the length of time that trauma sometimes continues in this broken world. We glimpse the extremes of pain that human beings can experience. We feel his loneliness, his abandonment, his fear. We can enter into the possibility that he might want to exert revenge on those who have hurt him once the balance of power changes. The story doesn't end there though . . . We can revel in his final conclusion: 'You intended to harm me, but God intended it for good' (Genesis 50:20). God did have a plan all along – his suffering may have been terrible, but through it, many lives were saved.

Some may respond, 'But I'm not going to be saving many lives, am I? Joseph was worth rescuing; I'm not.' It's a story that warms us up for the wonderful truths of Romans 8, that God brings (and indeed intends) good out of all situations faced by every single one of his children. That doesn't mean that God condones abuse – we will need to emphasize that abuse is sin, and abusers remain responsible for that sin – but it does mean there is hope of something better for all who are in Christ – both now and in eternity.

What about those who aren't believers? There are other characters to whom we can turn. In the New Testament, we can look at some of the tax collectors and sinners with whom Jesus ate. Zacchaeus was not one of society's upstanding characters. He was hated by the Jews as a collaborator and a cheat. Despised by the Romans as a minion of no real worth. Yet Jesus called him to follow him and changed his life around. Over the course of one extraordinary meal, Zacchaeus moved from being on the periphery of his people to being welcomed into God's eternal kingdom. There was nothing of merit about this little man, but Jesus used his power to bring transformation and hope. Then there is the woman at the well in John 4 – an outcast of her society with relationship struggles right at the heart of her experience. She too ended up being transformed by her encounter with the one who offers living water.

As we tell these stories (in the context of conversation or formal study), we can help those who are struggling to enter into the narrative: seeing who they are like, what God is like, and how things might just change.

A bigger God in poetry

It's not just in story that we find illustrations of the awesomeness of God; the Psalms too (which we encountered earlier) paint a wonderful picture. When walking alongside those who have been hurt, it can be worth taking a psalm – or a metaphor used in the Psalms – each week and reflecting on what it shows us about God. How does it transform us when we realize that the Lord is our God Almighty, dripping with authority and overflowing with power? What does it mean for him to be our stronghold or our defender? What difference does it make for us to have a refuge or a hiding place in him?

These are questions that can provoke some deep wrestling. Moving from thinking, 'God is a fortress, but he doesn't protect me' to a place of believing, 'I am welcome in God's fortress any time' rarely happens overnight, but it's a wonderful journey to go on.

At times, I use sheets like the one in Figure 1 overleaf: infographics that set out wonderful truths.[1] They're conversation starters, visual reminders, memory-verse joggers, which help the truths of God's Word to begin to seep in. They're just one way to help people see that God is sufficient for all their needs.

A bigger God at the cross

Ultimately, there is no better place to see the power and goodness of God than at the cross. There we find, in sacrificial wonder, the depths of God's love for us. There we see his victory over sin and death.

It's striking, however, that much talk of the cross can pass by those who have been abused.

All too often the death and resurrection of Jesus are pitched purely in terms of guilt washed away, and its benefits couched primarily in the ways his work opens up

HOW DO THE PSALMS DESCRIBE GOD?

A STRONGHOLD
PSALM 18:2

A SHIELD
PSALM 84:11

A FORTRESS
PSALM 91:2

A SHEPHERD
PSALM 23:1

THE MIGHTY ONE
PSALM 132:2

A DEFENDER
PSALM 68:5

A REFUGE
PSALM 46:1

THE living GOD
PSALM 42:2

LOVING GOD
PSALM 144:2

A HIDING-PLACE
PSALM 32:7

A ROCK
PSALM 19:14

THE LORD GOD ALMIGHTY
PSALM 89:8

Figure 1 How do the Psalms describe God?

the path to eternal life. Those things are precious beyond measure and unswervingly true, but they aren't always the aspects of the cross that need to be heard in every conversation.

At the fall, Adam and Eve's dishonouring attitudes and disobedient actions resulted in two major problems: guilt before God and separation from God. When Jesus died on the cross, those two age-old problems were reversed. As he took the punishment we deserved, we were declared innocent. As he made us clean, we were brought back into relationship with the Father and equipped to live in community with him.

If we talk about the cross purely in terms of forgiveness when walking alongside those who have been abused, we are at risk of two errors. We can create the impression that the abuse is their fault and they are in need of forgiveness for it. Or we can create the impression that, as they are not guilty (at least in regard to the abuse), then the cross has no relevance to cases of domestic violence – it only impacts on their (or their abuser's) sin.

If, however, in addition to forgiveness, we talk about Jesus' work on the cross as something that brings us close to God (no matter what our background), and gives us power to live for God (no matter what our present circumstances), then those who are being abused can better grasp the benefits of God's outrageous power and grace for the situations within their homes and hearts.

The cross used to confuse me. Worse than that, talk of it used to leave me feeling condemned. 'Isn't it exciting that our sins are washed away?' the preacher would say week after week. All I could hear was 'Great – Jesus is sorting it out so my abuser can be forgiven, and in the meantime I just carry on

*getting hit.' Don't get me wrong – I do know I need forgiveness
to the very core of my being. But when it came to my abuse,
I didn't need forgiving for that; I needed help to change
things. It wasn't until someone explained to me that the cross
helps those who are victims of sin as well as those who are
perpetrators of sin that talk of Jesus' death and resurrection
really connected with life at home.*

One practical way we can encourage people to grasp the
power and grace of God is to help them memorize Scripture.
Each month we can pick a different set of verses and learn
them together. Passages such as Colossians 1:15–20 are a
good place to start:

The Son is the image of the invisible God, the firstborn over
all creation. For in him all things were created: things in
heaven and on earth, visible and invisible, whether thrones
or powers or rulers or authorities; all things have been
created through him and for him. He is before all things,
and in him all things hold together. And he is the head of
the body, the church; he is the beginning and the firstborn
from among the dead, so that in everything he might have
the supremacy. For God was pleased to have all his fullness
dwell in him, and through him to reconcile to himself all
things, whether things on earth or things in heaven, by
making peace through his blood, shed on the cross.

**How should I read the Bible with someone who
is being abused?**
Those in situations of domestic abuse may find formal
Bible study hard. Some will be at their wits' end –
concentration is difficult when life is falling apart.

Others may be scared to respond to questions, fearful
of the consequences (or the feelings of failure) when
they get an answer wrong. In the early days, it can
be best simply to read (or even paraphrase) a short
narrative and draw out one truth about God or his world.

Next, you can try memory verses, encouraging people
to reflect on how remembering such truths impacts on
their lives. Later, it can be useful to treat Bible study as
an opportunity to curl up in a chair and hear from the
God who loves us, asking the person to read a short
passage aloud and saying what strikes them and what
difference that makes.

Eventually, it can be good to move on to reading
passages together and asking four simple questions:

1. What does this tell us about God?
2. What does this tell us about his world?
3. What does this tell us about people like us?
4. What difference does this make to the way we live?

Keeping the questions predictable from week to week
can take away the fear factor.

A bigger God who can be trusted

Grasping the power of God is much more than a theological
exercise. We want people to turn to him in their need.

Hosea 7:14 is a verse that can easily pass us by. It reads
simply:

They do not cry out to me from their hearts
  but wail on their beds.

Here is a reminder that, in the tough times, there are two ways to cry. Those who are hurting can cry on their beds – this is hopeless crying, crying that results in nothing but a damp pillow and red eyes. Alternatively, there is crying out to the Lord – that's hope-filled and hope-fuelled crying, crying that connects with the Maker of all things. The more people can see God as good and great, the more they will choose to cry out to him.

8 Changing mirrors

My next-door neighbours are quiz aficionados. They move from church to community centre month by month, frequently returning home victorious. Sometimes they take me along for the ride. Their general knowledge is astonishing – mine rather less so! Except, that is, when it comes to looking at distorted photos of Bond villains. It's a niche gift, I'll admit, but it's wonderful to be able to pinpoint someone's true identity amid great confusion.

New ID

Once those who are struggling begin to see the power and beauty of God, we can help them understand how he sees them. Why is this important? It is if we are to help them take off their old view of themselves as an unlovable piece of trash, without value or purpose, and put on a new identity as precious children of God, equipped to live for him. Ephesians 1 is a great chapter to help us explore that more.

The verses here remind us that all Christians are chosen children of the sovereign King – not in his kingdom by accident or default, but called there because of his great love. They remind us that God is not keeping believers at arm's length, but holding us close, lavishing us with grace and blessing us with every spiritual blessing in the heavenly realms. All who are in Christ have the Holy Spirit as a deposit, guaranteeing that we are in his kingdom and will be for ever. Christians who are abused can be sure of that: those blessings are poured into them because Jesus is worth it, and he has chosen them to share in his blessings. Non-Christians can be invited to explore the invitation that lies within.

Taken in over time, there is real balm here for the soul, and beauty that can turn people's worlds the right way up. Rather than assuming they can't have a close relationship with God because they're useless, they can see that intimacy is possible because of Jesus. Rather than imagining they are guilty, they can see there is no condemnation for those in Christ. They can begin to glimpse the privileges of kingdom life: a life of closeness, eternity and safety.

Remembering it all can be a bit of a challenge, so in Figure 2 is an aide-memoire that will help. After explaining each facet, it can be useful to provide a summary sheet[1] to help sufferers reflect each day on who God has made them to be.

WHAT IS TRUE
OF ME WHEN I AM A
CHRISTIAN **?**

GUARANTEED
AN INHERITANCE
EPHESIANS 1:14

PREDESTINED TO BE
ADOPTED
EPHESIANS 1:5

CHOSEN
BEFORE THE
BEGINNING OF TIME
EPHESIANS 1:4

CALLED
TO BE HOLY
& **BLAMELESS**
EPHESIANS 1:4

LAVISHED
WITH
GRACE
EPHESIANS 1:8

FORGIVEN MY
SINS
EPHESIANS 1:7

INCLUDED IN CHRIST
EPHESIANS 1:13

REDEEMED
THROUGH HIS BLOOD EPHESIANS 1:7

BLESSED WITH EVERY
SPIRITUAL BLESSING
EPHESIANS 1:3

loved
EPHESIANS 1:4

SEALED
WITH THE PROMISED
HOLY SPIRIT
EPHESIANS 1:13

GIVEN
PEACE
EPHESIANS 1:2

Figure 2 What is true of me when I am a Christian?

But what if someone has a victim mentality that just won't shift?

Some who have been abused are so used to being a victim of someone else's anger that they cannot see themselves in any other light. They may be individuals who seem deliberately to put themselves in danger, people who get embroiled in multiple abusive relationships within and outside the family. Even when the light of Scripture is brought to bear on their lives, they seem to cling on to the darkness and a view of themselves that is unswervingly unbiblical – they are committed to seeing themselves through the lens of victimhood and find little appeal in moving on. Often such people don't know they're doing this. Pointing it out may be necessary, but is unlikely to be received well. Prayerful perseverance here is the only answer, allowing truth to drip in for years (decades if necessary). Humanly impossible situations are perfectly possible for God.

Facing such resistance to change can be hugely frustrating. There may be times when those of us helping the abused may need to spur one another on. It's important that we don't give up. People who are being abused have often been abandoned before, and walking away will only cause further pain. However, we may also need to be wise with our time. Sometimes it's best to reduce meetings to monthly or bimonthly until the person involved is genuinely ready to embrace the process of change.

New way to be

As time progresses, the building blocks begin to fall into place. If the Lord is sovereign and good, there is hope for the future. If the abused are precious in the sight of the Lord, it's worth pursuing change.

The final building block flows from 2 Peter 1:3: 'His divine power has given us everything we need for a godly life through our knowledge of him who called us by his own glory and goodness.'

The wonderful truth of this verse needs to ring out with clarity: no matter what abuse has been faced in the past, no matter what traumas we face in the present, Christians are equipped to live differently in the future.

This is no call to revolution. This is not a motivational text designed to encourage people to go home, irresponsibly confront their abusers and demand that things change. The strength that God provides needs to be used wisely and in community. It is a confident assertion, however, that God equips his children to keep following him, even through the most difficult paths of change.

Those facing abuse need to hear that they don't have to seek change in their own strength, and that, in Christ, they are able to walk towards a new way of living. If they leave home (temporarily or for ever) – if the abuser is removed from the home (temporarily or for ever) – they still have what they need to keep going. It will be hard, but it's possible.

Did the early believers ever claim their rights?

The Christian way is a life of sacrifice. In the pages of Scripture we see many people willing to undergo great hardship for the sake of the gospel. Those who have been abused sometimes see that they are equipped to live differently, but still choose to stay as an act of 'sacrifice'. It's important to draw out distinctions between self-sacrifice that progresses the gospel and sacrifice that merely colludes with an abuser's desires. It can also be helpful to show that this new way of being can involve asking for justice. Paul understood sacrifice: he was arrested, flogged, imprisoned and shipwrecked (2 Corinthians 11:24–25), but he also, at times, sought recourse in law. Acts 16:37 is an intriguing verse. After being unjustly whipped, he publicly pointed out that he had been criminally mistreated. A life of sacrifice is not a life devoid of recourse to the law.

New words of praise

It may not sound like a priority when someone is being abused, but encouraging people to praise can be transformational. There's something wonderful about singing facts rather than just thinking them in the quietness of our heart. Putting voice to what the Bible says helps truth sink in, and it injects real emotion into doctrine. Someone who is genuinely praising God for his greatness is more likely to trust that greatness for the change to come.

There needs to be a note of caution here. We mustn't give the impression that God's provision of himself, and the resulting perspective and strength, in any way guarantee protection from the abuse at home. The people whom we are supporting still live in a broken world – they are still, at this point, likely to be embroiled in a volatile and dangerous environment.

With this caveat in place, however, we can encourage people to sing out their praise to the God who saves, offers a continuous equipping, enables them in the present, and promises eternal safety in the life to come. A song, written and sung in my home church, has spoken powerfully into the lives of those struggling in this area. It's a glorious reminder that, in Christ, there is joy and hope fuelled by his steadfast love even in the darkest of times. Why not play it in a meeting? Let the wonder sink in:

If I have fled to Jesus,
Found refuge in his care.
What enemy can breach these walls
And turn my joy to fear?
Has he not promised good to me?
Will then his promise fail?
Will he prove absent-minded
And my enemy prevail?

If all things hold together
In Jesus Christ, the Son,
Sustained by his almighty word
That cannot be undone,
If even sparrows catch his eye
Why should I doubt my place?
Why should I stop to question
If he holds me in his grace?

If God appoints his blessing
To fall on rebel ground,
His sun to shine and rain to fall
Where thanks are never found,
If even my ungrateful heart
He sought and reconciled
Why doubt he will embrace me
Now that he has called me 'child'?

If Jesus' blood is precious
God's treasured, only Son
Yet God allowed that blood to flow
Till all his wrath was done,
If on the cross I see such love
How can I be unsure?
What else could he be planning
But to love forevermore?[2]

Section 3

ENCOURAGING
PRACTICAL CHANGE

9 Into the light

It took over a year to get to the point where I thought change might be possible. It took many more months to see this as desirable. I can't even begin to remember how many times my friends at church had to tell me that God loved me before it sank in. Eventually, it started to make a difference though. Little by little, I came to understand that God didn't want me to live in fear of abuse. I came to understand that I didn't have to hate my husband, I didn't even have to divorce him, but I did have to take significant action if things were ever going to change. Simply trying harder was never going to make a difference. Hoping for the best was a road to nowhere. Real change means real action.

When the moment of asking for help to take action arrives, it's a cause for celebration. We can praise God for building up a precious person to the point of realization that abuse is wrong and hope is real. It's a moment that always makes me smile.

It is also a moment for caution though. We need to be careful, because those who have been abused find it easy, soon after, to backtrack and abandon the quest for change. We need to be cautious, because an abused person is never more at risk than when beginning to move towards a position where the abuser no longer has power.

Next steps

It's hard to imagine now, but when I was in my teens I used to love hiking in the wild. With a pack on my back, a map in my hand and a group of friends at my side, I used to wander through the Brecon Beacons or other British delights. It was exciting trekking into the unknown. It wasn't something I was allowed to do on a whim though, nor was it something I entered into unprepared. My expedition instructors instilled in me the importance of wearing suitable footwear, packing the right gear, fuelling up on energy-giving foods, and knowing how to keep safe if (or should that be, when) I got lost. I can still hear one of their favourite catchphrases ringing in my head: 'A safe expedition is a planned expedition.'

The same applies to those embarking on the journey of change within the family home.

Finance is a key area that will need some thought. Now might be the moment to establish a separate bank account (ensuring that statements are sent somewhere secure). It's also the time when we can consider what help, as a church, we can give to those about to leave. Can we set aside a grant, for example, to help cover costs?

Important documents can usefully be removed to a secure location – possibly the church safe. If those who are planning to leave can hand over their passport, birth certificate, marriage certificate, National Insurance details, prescriptions and driver's licence to one of the people walking alongside them, this will mean it will be easier to access help in the coming months. If we encourage this – and please give them a receipt – it provides a measure of protection if the abuser finds out and launches accusations of theft.

If we want to give the abused planning for the future a gift, a new pay-as-you-go phone may be the best idea. This provides a method of communicating that the abuser knows nothing about.

And whilst it's not wise to remove too many obvious objects from the home, as doing so may arouse suspicion, items of particular sentimental value (a mother's locket or a precious photo) should be put somewhere safe. It means that when the time comes for the abused person or the abuser to leave home, no important objects can get destroyed, even if things become violent for a while.

But what happens when people change their mind?

The path to freedom from domestic abuse is rarely straight. People who are being abused can ebb and flow in their desire to leave. There may be numerous occasions when they say they want things to change, but then back out. Such fear must never be met by condemnation, only encouragement to try again.

No one rebukes a toddler for faltering when taking those first stumbling steps. So it is with those who are attempting to live abuse-free for the first time in years.

Separate ways

One of the most common 'backtrack' questions I hear is: 'OK, I'm ready for change, but instead of leaving or involving the law, can't we just work it out while we're all still living under the same roof?' The answer is simple: 'No, not unless the abuse is in its very early stages and at the very mild end of the spectrum – it just doesn't work.'

It's important to remember that situations of domestic abuse are not cases where two sinful human beings need to do things a little bit differently. They are contexts in which one person has a legacy of manipulation and pain that contravenes the law, and the other person (or people) has been repeatedly hurt to the extent that it has impacted on life in a significant way.

It is possible for an abuser to change – with God all things are possible. And it is not always essential to live apart for ever. Indeed, where abuse is not yet an ingrained pattern, the time apart can be reasonably short (if that is what both parties genuinely want). However, an abuser who has been causing significant damage over a sustained period of time won't stop manipulating and hurting overnight. Those individuals will need substantial input if they are to live differently. Change is hard, and the process of transformation will probably involve both moments of significant growth and moments of substantial relapse. As we saw earlier, if the person who has been abused stays living with the abuser, then the abuse will almost inevitably continue in some form. That is not acceptable.

There are only two options: either the abuser needs to leave the home, or the person being abused needs to leave. For the abuser to leave, it is almost always necessary to involve some representatives of the law. Often this will be specially trained police officers, who will gather evidence, take statements and speak to witnesses before arresting the person causing the hurt. Such action can be planned carefully. It can take place when any children are at school or clubs. Police are often willing to pick a time for the arrest that causes the least risk to those who have been victims of crime. After questioning, the person accused of abuse may be charged, and might be bailed with specific restrictions that prevent them from approaching the home and the people they have been hurting. A mutual friend, sometimes under police escort, may be allowed back into the home to pick up some of the abuser's belongings. If abusers breach bail conditions, they can be arrested again. In the fullness of time (and if the Crown Prosecution Service makes the decision to proceed), they could well face prosecution and a criminal record.

At other times, people can seek protection orders or injunctions that will be served on those accused of abuse. These orders can prevent abusers from approaching those they have been hurting, or coming to the family home. A trained solicitor will be able to guide people through the process.

Often these steps are enough to ensure security. Bail conditions and protection orders, however, are sometimes breached. It's crucial that the one who has been abused is encouraged not to 'make an exception and meet up for a bit'. It's important to ensure that the person who has been hurt is willing to call the police (or ask others to call) if he or she is approached by the abuser. To put an order in position but then welcome an abuser back into the home puts the person who has suffered abuse at even greater risk.

For the abused person to leave, it is often necessary to involve professionals who can advise on housing options, finance, protection orders and so on. Domestic abuse hotlines and organizations such as Victim Support often act as a one-stop shop for such information, or can, at least, refer the abused on to agencies that may be able to assist. If paperwork needs to change hands, it can be safest to route forms via a neutral address, such as the church.

It is essential to discern how much it is wise to discuss with any children in the home. Young children should not be informed of the plans to move. Older teenagers may be informed, but it's important not to put big decisions on their shoulders – they are to be protected, not given extra burdens.

Once new accommodation has been found, bags can be packed quickly. It's important not to alert the abuser to the fact that family members are about to leave – that will often result in anger or further acts of control. We can encourage people to pack only the essentials: clothes, key documents (if they aren't already somewhere safe), items of real sentimental value and useful technology. Other items can be reclaimed or replaced at a later date.

It's vital that they aim to leave the home at a time when the abuser is not about. It is sometimes possible to arrange for the police to be present, just in case the abuser returns. A pre-booked cab or a friend's car can whisk them away to their new home.

Once safe, it's time to inform key people what has been going on:

- The wider family will be concerned, and it's important they know their loved ones are OK. It's not essential for every family member to be given the new address.

The fewer people who know, the fewer there will
be to be manipulated into passing on information.

- Family doctors will need to know the new address
  and be alert to the need for support in the coming
  weeks. This might include being a listening ear,
  referring the children on to specialist services, or
  the provision of antidepressant medication to help
  navigate the pain within.
- Schools and childminders will need to be aware and
  have clear instructions on what they can and cannot
  tell should the other parent call (and who is allowed
  to pick up the children now).
- Employers can usefully be kept in the loop – not least
  so that they are alert to the possibility of the abuser
  turning up and asking awkward questions.

Other than that, information sharing should be limited.
That means avoiding giving out locations to those who
don't need to know, but it also involves being mindful of
the kinds of social media posts put up by adults, friends
and children alike. A picture with a geotag (that is, a tag
that assigns a geographical location to a photo or video)
can easily be used by an abuser to track someone down
and inflict even more pain.

> **What about the pets?**
> Abusers don't always limit themselves to hurting other
> humans. Sometimes animals in the home suffer too.
> It can be hard to run and leave them behind, knowing
> what they might suffer as a result. Not many refuges
> will take pets. A few will accommodate a hamster or
> gerbil in a cage, but anything that runs free is unlikely

to find a home there or in council-sourced emergency accommodation. It is still worth removing them from the home, if possible, though. Maybe a friend can take them in? Alternatively, charities like Dogs Trust run projects to help those fleeing domestic abuse.

The process of moving can be hard. Leaving behind a way of life, even a way that has been profoundly painful, is never easy. Once living somewhere safe, however, the task of rebuilding can begin.

10 Brand-new lives

'Go on – round you go.' It was the dreaded warm-up game at the start of team-building day. 'You've got to spin around twelve times!' I was feeling dizzy after just two. There was no escaping the activity though; no way I could let down my group. So I drew a breath and followed the rules: turn around in a circle a dozen times, then run towards the next member of your team wearing a giant foam hand . . . You can imagine the scene: eyes, legs, torso, all trying to go their own way. Disorientation in the extreme. After a while, I decided all I could do was sit until the chaos in my mind had passed.

It can be easy to assume that leaving an abusive relationship might bring some relief. To some it does, in small measure at least. For others, the fear, the adrenaline rush, the new surroundings, the new people now involved in their life can bring profound confusion.

Changing practicalities

Leaving home is tough. There are many practical questions that will need answering in the first few weeks. Where does the local bus go? How does the central heating turn on? How will I get to work? Can I trust my new neighbours? It's important to allow time to adjust.

Friends from church can play a significant part in helping those who've fled navigate through the practicalities that lie ahead. It's important, as we should know by now, not to give out the new address to everyone in the congregation – discretion is key – but if a small group of trusted friends can spend time popping round to help in the process of orientation, that can be invaluable.

Those who have been abused may not have had the freedom to handle their own finances for a long time, so the concept of budgeting may be hard. They may not have had the freedom to choose curtains in the past, having to live constantly under the control of others. The simple act of going shopping, and having to exercise choice, can be simultaneously exhilarating and terrifying. Having a friend alongside can make all the difference.

How can I keep on supporting them if they move miles away?

Sometimes people move in with family members who live at a distance. Sometimes they are placed in refuges in a different county. It can feel hard to keep in contact, but there is still much that we can do:

- Keep praying
- Keep texting verses of Scripture

- Keep visiting (even if it is only once a month, it can be a great encouragement for people to have a date in the diary)
- Keep liaising (get in touch with a local church and see if someone from that congregation can give the person a call).

Remaining in the family home is often just as hard as leaving.

Like the person above who needs to learn to budget, someone who has been controlled may have little idea of how to pay the utility bills. In the past, they have been accused of being too stupid to undertake a responsibility like that. Who can help them make the calls? Who will go to the bank and explain what's going on?

If someone has had to go on state benefits for the first time, there might be meetings and forms to navigate, many of which take time to process. Who can be the trusted figure who helps the survivor of abuse to liaise well with all the agencies involved?

Then, of course, there is the matter of legal proceedings. If charges have been brought against the perpetrator, is there someone in the congregation who can go along to court? Is there a group of people who can pray?

Can the church liaise with statutory agencies?
The safeguarding officer is likely to be the first person at church to liaise with social services when abuse comes to light, and will work through the referral process with the statutory services and ensure that information flows. That person may continue in a liaison role for quite some time.

However, the safeguarding officer may not be the right person to liaise with housing officers, GPs, social workers, teachers, Victim Support and other agencies over the months (or years) that follow. If that individual steps back, it is worth having another 'point person' at church who can liaise with those professionals involved. This might include passing on ongoing concerns about the struggling person, inviting advisers to come to the church for meetings, and listening to advice from specialists in the field. This point person is often the pastor, someone with a professional title and role that makes it easier for social workers and solicitors to understand and interact with – but it doesn't have to be.

Due to the confidentiality constraints of many professions, it may not always be possible for social workers to tell ministers what is happening, but they are often keen to listen, and it is a good idea to build up relationships with them. Statutory bodies often value the input of faith groups.

Changing emotions

On an emotional level, questions abound. Should I have left him? Will he come after me? Whom can I trust? She may be out of my house, but will she ever be out of my head? The cords that bind people together are not broken by mere geography.

Sometimes the first few weeks away are filled with tears. Abusers may cause pain, but they are often loved too. The absence of bruises can feel like small consolation for being parted from someone you adore.

At the other extreme, an outpouring of anger may occur. Years of frustration, previously suppressed by fear, can unleash itself, taking everyone by surprise. 'How could he have done that to me?' a sufferer cries. For a few, post-traumatic stress symptoms can begin to arise.

Self-rebuke is common. 'Why didn't I leave earlier? Why was I so stupid?' A catalogue of what-if scenarios can be rehearsed. Parents can convince themselves that they've done their children irreparable harm by not moving sooner.

For some, the weeks immediately after leaving are largely numb. Shock can set in. No anger, no joy, nothing.

The church can play an important role here too. Giving people the chance to express these emotions can be hugely helpful. Listening to their stories, longings and losses can be a real act of love. Affirming people in some of those emotions is important too. Loss should be met with tears. Anger is a right response to abuse.

Pouring out such emotions to God in prayer is a helpful avenue too. The psalmists didn't hold back their feelings, but allowed them to flow in a Godward direction rather than spilling them out elsewhere. They were good at articulating, 'This hurts – but I trust you, Lord.' Encouraging people to process their emotions in that way can be an immense help, and, as we have already seen, the Psalms can provide words for those who don't know what to say.

Sometimes emotions will need to be challenged. We don't need to stop people speaking, but we can help them discern which emotions are flowing from a right heart and which are flowing from a wayward one. Anger is right, but a desire for revenge is not. Grief for loss is right, but a decision that life is no longer worth living is not.

Confusion is reasonable, but the conclusion that life was better before is far from true.

At times like these, it can be useful to look at stories such as Exodus 16. Enslaved for years, the Israelites suffered much at the hands of the Egyptians. It took a long time for them to escape. When they did, they regretted it almost instantly. There was more food back in Egypt, they wailed! In their words we hear deep fear of the future. We also hear deep rebellion in their desire to turn their back on what God had done for them and return to slavery and abuse once more. Allowing people to see themselves in the narrative of Exodus can be an enlightening process. Seeing God's gracious provision in those pages, even in the face of doubt and fear, can bring further hope.

Changing spiritual questions

Spiritual matters are no easier to navigate:

> As I was packing my bags, I knew I had no choice: I had to get out of the house. He had beaten me repeatedly, and he was starting to threaten the kids. A mother's instinct kicked in – I had to get my family to safety. But as I was unpacking in my new flat, the certainty ebbed away. Maybe it hadn't been as bad as I remembered? Maybe I was better off back home? Maybe I wouldn't be able to cope without him? Maybe God was angry? I mean, I'm a Christian. I promised to love, honour and obey. I knew, when I made the promise, that it was meant to stick even when life was hard. My vows were 'until death parts'. We were both alive – had I committed some terrible sin?

The weeks following a big change can be fraught with doubts and questions. Is this really what God wants? Haven't I messed up God's plan for marriage now I've walked away? Aren't I breaking the commandment to honour my parents now that I've left the man they chose for me? Maybe I should just have turned the other cheek? The gentle balm of good theology will be needed day by day. This may be a period when some of the biblical truths explored earlier need to be visited afresh.

Can we remind sufferers that honouring our parents doesn't mean letting people get away with abuse? Loving our parents, in part, means helping them become like Christ through good boundaries, and enabling them to find better ways of relating to their adult children.

Can we repeat the fact that turning the other cheek doesn't mean silence in the face of injustice? There may be times when we choose, for the glory of God, to suffer, but there should never be times when we choose to suffer for the convenience of an abuser. Scripture is littered with examples of people who escaped trauma, and we can let those stories drip from our lips. David ran away from Saul when his life was in danger. He didn't say, 'God's in charge. I just need to take it.' Esther risked her life to save herself and her people from being wiped out. She didn't quietly accept the death sentence to come. They followed God, not their tormentor's will.

Marriage doesn't negate the law. We all accept that the law of the land has the right to incarcerate a man who has attacked a stranger. Romans 13 reminds us that we are subject to those laws. That includes accepting that it is right for a man (or a woman) to be incarcerated for beating a spouse.

We should never be afraid humbly and sensitively to repeat what is true. We all need reminding of God's Word on a regular basis.

Confronting the abuser

Abusers who have been removed from the home by police will have been confronted with their crimes. They may not, however, have been confronted with the fact that their actions are an affront to God. It can be helpful for a pastor (and another member of the congregation of the same gender as the abuser) to offer to meet with the one who has been told to leave. (If this doesn't happen, these big life changes might end up being processed without God.) Like all pastoral meetings, this can involve listening, praying, opening Scripture and speaking words of comfort. It is, however, first and foremost likely to be a meeting where the abuser is confronted with their sin and called to repent and participate in biblical – or secular – counselling that teases out why they tend towards control, and how they can stop unleashing their frustrations on others.

If the abused has left the family home, the abuser may be confused as to why. A similar pastoral visit explaining the situation and talking about Jesus' grace and power for change may be necessary.

The whirlwind of change can be a challenging experience, but one that is laced with hope. With those involved in places of safety and receiving gospel-centred help, the scene is now set for true and lasting change.

11 Looking to the future

I am not a fan of flying. Not a fan at all. If you're wondering how deeply that sentiment goes, I recently took a twenty-one-hour train journey back from Poland. Sharing a couchette with an all-night chanter seemed preferable to fastening a seatbelt and preparing to taxi to runway 1. For years, I kept that particular quirk hidden. I'd say I didn't like overseas holidays; I'd spout (not illegitimate) environmental qualms about getting on a plane. I thought that it would be easier if no one could see my foibles and fears. I was wrong. There's real joy in knowing that people are praying for me on those rare occasions when I give 35,000 feet a whirl – there's real blessing in letting others see my frailty and my need of them.

Suddenly everyone knew. For years, the abuse had been my dirty little secret. For months, only the vicar and my closest friend had been part of the plan to leave. But now the kids and I were alone in the house. My husband was miles away,

banned from contacting us, banned from coming to church.
It wasn't a secret any more. I was scared about how people
would react.

Once an abuser has been removed from the family home,
or left behind while others move on, there is no more pretending that everything is OK.

Some prefer the news to trickle out naturally, as conversations happen between family and friends. Others
would rather have some limited kind of announcement
where the minister talks to, or emails, those in church who
really need to know: the small group leader, the children's
group leaders, the elders and the stewards who welcome
people on the door (who may need to ask the abuser to
leave).

If both the abuser and the abused go to the same
church, there will be an inevitable need for one of them,
preferably the abuser, to move for a while at least. It is
impossible for them to have the space from one another
that they need if they are seeing each other once or twice
a week.

It is virtually impossible for leadership teams to
support both parties well – far better to enlist the help of
others from a nearby church which teaches the Bible well.
There will be a need to brief the other pastor effectively
and ensure that the church has enough information to be
able to nurture and hold the abuser to account.

This doesn't mean that the original church leaders need
to cut off one of the parties – lines of communication and
love can keep on flowing – it just means that it's best to
share the responsibilities of care.

How can the church help those who have been abused
to move forwards?

Looking to community

It may have been a while since the abused last had good friends. Honesty and openness don't thrive in abusive homes. Step by step, it is important to help people rebuild trust with the wider church community and beyond.

Building trust is no easy task. People may share some of their story with you and then shut you out. This isn't capriciousness at play; it's an indication of how hard it is to share something personal and how tempting it can be to run away in fear once that sharing has taken place.

Children too will need to learn how to be friends without keeping scary secrets. Explaining to them the difference between a good secret (a surprise party) and a bad secret (not telling when someone is getting hurt) will be key.

Community can be particularly important when people come from cultures where battling abuse runs against the grain. It's not unknown for battered wives (or indeed husbands) to be shunned by their families and friends for deciding to leave the family home. It's seen as an issue of shame and dishonour. Inviting people round for a few hours every couple of months won't help them see what true friendship is like. We – and a group of others – need to be in regular (although sustainable) contact with those we are seeking to support.

Looking to boundaries

Those who have been controlled for many years may struggle to understand boundaries. Their relationships within the home may have been one of two extremes: shunned and called useless on a regular basis, but spending every waking hour trying to please the one they loved and feared. That style of relating can easily get transferred on to new friends.

> *I used to shower my friends with gifts. I wanted them to like me and I wasn't sure they would. Showing them how much they meant to me by buying them stuff felt like a helpful way to go. I wasn't trying to buy their love, just make sure they felt mine. After a while, it got too much for them. I guess they felt awkward, as it's not what friends usually do (I now know). They asked me to stop buying them things. That sentence felt like a punch in the gut. I was giving love. I was receiving rejection. It was like the abuse was happening all over again. I cried for hours. It wasn't until someone sat me down and explained how friendships work that I began to see I wasn't loving them, and they weren't rejecting me.*

We can talk to people about what friendship is like. We can look at examples such as David and Jonathan, or Paul and Timothy, to see how to navigate the ups and downs of relationships in a fallen world. There we will find encouragements to love and loyalty, reminders of human fallibility, examples of how to spur one another on.

Another area to address may be helping people to say 'no'. It may have been impossible to say that to the one who has abused – the retribution was just too severe. Learning that it's not only safe to say 'no', but good too, may be a complete bolt from the blue.

The reconciliation question

As the months proceed, a call will need to be made on whether or not contact is going to be resumed with the person who has perpetrated the abuse.

If the abuser is unrepentant and has made no effort to change, then resuming any kind of relationship will undoubtedly be unwise. If there are children involved, there may have to be some contact (although this can be indirect, through mediators, solicitors or social workers and the decisions of family courts), but in all other respects it is best to keep far away. It's all too easy to fall back into old habits and allow the abuse to resume.

Moving away from family can be hard. It may mean sacrificing family gatherings for the foreseeable future. On the other hand, if the decision to attend such events is made, it's prudent to make sure the one who has suffered much does not go alone or unsupported. Prayer will be needed before attending. It can be useful to think through likely scenarios, such as how to respond if the person is verbally cruel or utterly charming.

Afterwards a debrief will probably be necessary. Such encounters can provoke strong reactions.

If the abuser is repentant but struggling to change, here too distance is wise. Just as alcoholics recover best when they stay away from their friends who drink, and gamblers persevere best away from their betting shop buddies, so abusers tend to grow best away from those they used to abuse. It's wise to remember that God can bring others into their life to do the encouraging.

There are exceptions. In controlled, restorative justice scenarios, it can be helpful to both parties for the person who has been hurt to set out just how painful a family member's actions have been. In carefully guided sessions, pain can be expressed, and tormentors constructively confronted with the devastation they have caused. It's not something to enter into lightly, however. Both parties need to be ready for the sessions to come.

At other times, full reconciliation can be sought, and how beautiful when it works! If someone who has abused in the past is genuinely repentant, and has engaged well with appropriate help, then there is hope for the future. There can be some joint counselling (to practise new styles of relating) and a trial period of reconciliation. If this goes well, a permanent restoration may bring great joy to all involved. There will need to be ongoing accountability (and anyone who is truly repentant will embrace that accountability), but in some cases families can indeed come together again.

How is it possible to tell that it is safe to live with someone again? Asking these questions of abusers (and those who are standing alongside) may help:

- Have they grown in their relationship with God, turning to him in their need rather than demanding help from others?
- Have they grown in their understanding of themselves, being able to articulate better their desires, strengths and weaknesses?
- Have they grown in their ability to express emotions well: can they say when they are hurt, lonely or frustrated without manipulating others and causing pain?
- Have they grown in humility, acknowledging where they are wrong and being willing to be guided by others?

- Have they grown in their independence, allowing family members to disagree with them and lead lives that are close but not intertwined?

Any attempt at reconciliation should take place only if both parties are committed to acting differently in the months ahead, and are willing to do so with the full support of their believing community from whom accountability will flow.

Is domestic violence grounds for divorce?

Marriage matters. It is a covenant relationship designed to last until death. Abuse matters. The psalmists remind us:

> The LORD examines the righteous,
>   but the wicked, those who love violence,
> he hates with a passion.
> (Psalm 11:5)

There can be a tension when abuse occurs in a marriage. Should the parties divorce or not? The Bible sets out two scenarios where divorce is clearly permissible. The first is where there has been some sexual infidelity (Matthew 5), and the second is where an unbeliever has abandoned his or her spouse (1 Corinthians 7). Both passages have an ethos of protection and wanting the good of those involved, rather than trying to be punitive or restrictive. Neither commands what has to be done. It is worth asking, though, where these cases of sexual infidelity or spousal abandonment might fit with domestic abuse.

If a spouse has repeatedly used pornography for sexual gratification, and done so in ways that deliberately and maliciously wound his wife, is that infidelity? If a spouse, who shows no sign of repentance, has been incarcerated for grievous bodily harm or attempted murder, is that abandonment by someone who cannot really be classed as a believer no matter what label he chooses to adopt for himself? Divorce is not a decision to be taken lightly. It is best decided with wise counsel from church leaders and mature friends. It should, however, be discussed. And if someone decides to divorce even when the church suspects there is a chance of reconciliation, this is not the unforgivable sin. Love and grace are the necessary responses, not condemnation. It's appropriate too to reflect on passages such as Deuteronomy 24:1–4. God doesn't encourage people to go back into wayward relationships once they've ended. That's for the good of all involved.

With Christian brothers and sisters at their side, boundaries firmly in place, and wise decisions about the future of the relationship beginning to form, there is no reason why those who have been abused can't go forward into the future, confident of the Lord's good provision for their lives. The legacy of abuse doesn't disappear overnight, but the possibility of true freedom is not far from sight.

12 Fallout and freedom

Trains are a big feature of my life (and not only when I'm avoiding airports like the plague!). I commute to work. I use them to get to church. They tend to be my chosen form of transport for relaxing weekends away. Given that I spend so much time on them, it's probably to be expected that I have a few embarrassing tales to tell. Moments when I've fallen asleep, moments when I've met some of life's more interesting characters, moments when I've made a complete fool of myself.

It was a rainy morning in 2016. I was late for work and, hearing the train pulling in, I bounded up to the platform as fast as my (thoroughly out-of-condition) lungs would permit. I leapt on to the train just as the doors were closing, ignoring the health and safety advice put out every day. The floor was wet. My shoes had no grip. Within a second, I was flat on my back, sliding down the aisle, with the good old British public averting their gaze. It was an impressive fall, if I say so myself. The sound of my body hitting the floor shocked even me.

Like any good commuter, I picked myself up, made a suitably self-effacing quip and continued on my journey, pretending everything was OK. Everything, however, was not OK. My elbow was cracked and swollen to the point of being stuck.

The NHS did their work well. Within hours, I was patched up and ready to go. Full function has since returned to my battered limb. It's never been quite the same though. The odd ache, the occasional twinge, especially on cold, wet days. It may have healed, but it's 'scarred' on the inside. I expect I'll be conscious of that for the rest of my life.

Whether someone decides to keep their distance from an abusive family member, or chooses to reconcile, the effects of abuse will not disappear overnight. Some won't disappear at all. In the years ahead, there will be battles to be fought and challenges to overcome.

Damaged goods?

I am so grateful to God for the way he changed my life. I was never physically hurt, but I was verbally battered for years – rendered too scared to leave the house. The Lord enabled me to move from near captivity to complete freedom. He surrounded me with wonderful friends. He brought me into contact with lovely social workers who helped me reach my new home. My daughter and I are now safe. My partner, who had caused so much pain, now has no contact with us at all. Life is great.

I've been trying to rebuild my life, so I decided to start internet dating a while ago. I've met some really nice guys.

*They didn't seem bothered by my past, but I can't quite seem
to get over it. I'm damaged stock, aren't I? No one in their right
mind should take a risk on me.*

God washes away the stains of the past, but we don't forget
the pain. The things that have been inflicted on those who
have been abused can engender feelings of being someone
else's cast-off, someone whose previous relationship failed.
Like clothes in a charity shop, they may have some beauty,
but everyone else can see they're not shiny and new.

That's not what the Bible says! According to Scripture,
they, like every other believer, are a new creation: the old
has gone, completely washed away (2 Corinthians 5:17).
No sin committed by a believer, no sin committed against
a believer, can change that loveliness. That fact was true
while the abuse was happening; it's true once the abuse
comes to an end. Helping people to remember that,
helping them to live in the light of that, is an important
place to dwell.

Unexpectedly alone

For those whose marriage (or other partnership) has been
destroyed by abuse, there can be significant wrestling with
the fact that they are now 'alone'. They shouldn't be isolated,
not if the church is rallying round (and committed to per-
severing in love in the months and years ahead), but they
are now without a significant family member. This isn't how
they were expecting life to be. It's one of the disappoint-
ments that reflecting on abuse can bring. Many people
struggle with this singleness, for it feels like a second-class
life. But the Bible has a far better perspective.

We don't quite know the backstory of the apostle Paul. We do know that to have been on the Sanhedrin, he must have been married at some stage. We know too that when he met Jesus on the road to Damascus, his wife was no longer around. It may well have been a painful parting, possibly a bereavement in the early years. He doesn't see that as a curse, though, but rather as an opportunity. It's a context that may well have been hard for him, but one that enables him to serve God well.

God has prepared good works for each of his children (Ephesians 2:10). In his wise and sovereign design, the plans he has for people who have lost their spouse as a result of abuse are for them to flourish in the absence of the one who has caused much pain. These are not his reserve plans – the ones that only come into play when plan A has crashed and burned – they are his good plans, ones that enable his children to prosper in his kingdom. The church can help people embrace this new way of being by ensuring that there are plenty of events and activities where single people feel welcome, and that there are people ready to babysit or childmind so that those who are starting over again can attend at least a few evening meetings at church.

Running in the wrong direction

Those who have been through abuse once can struggle in two different directions when the abuse is over. If they haven't really seen the true glories of God, the true horrors of abuse, the real vulnerabilities of their heart and the real wonder of their identity in Christ, they may be tempted to fall into a new abusive relationship. It's not that they are actively seeking abuse; it is that they are used to abuse. It feels familiar, and familiar is more comfortable than new.

After the abuse is over, it is wise for us as a church to get alongside sufferers and help them discern what their vulnerabilities may be:

- Is their desire for a partner so strong that they are tempted to run towards anyone who will now have them? We can remind them that longing for love is no bad thing, but that wanting love so much that we are willing to find it in all the wrong places is what the Bible calls idolatry, something that will drag them away from God and his perfect ways.
- Is their desire for security so strong that they are tempted to run towards material things? Maybe they have known great deprivation as part of the abuse and don't want to experience that again. We can reflect on the fact that wanting security is right and proper, but storing up treasures in heaven is a far better use of their time than storing up treasures on earth (Matthew 6:19–21).
- Is their desire for comfort so strong that they are tempted to run towards anyone who seems to be able to understand their pain? It's not wrong to want comfort. As we know, God is the 'God of all comfort' (2 Corinthians 1:3), and he loves to lavish his compassion on his children, but if we think we need to receive it first and foremost from another human being, then it will be easy to run into the arms of another who offers tenderness in the initial weeks, but reverts to pain in the months that follow.

On the other hand, some people will desire peace so much that they are resistant to trying a relationship with anyone else. It's not wrong to want peace. It's not wrong to choose a lifetime of singleness and celibacy. Those desires need to honour God though. If they are motivated purely by fear of the past repeating itself, then there is still processing to do. People will grow towards maturity best if they are encouraged to trust God and trust others more.

Struggling children

One of the biggest concerns expressed by parents who have escaped abuse is the impact it will have on the children, something that we touched on earlier. Many children and young people seem very resilient at the time. They can come across as happy and calm on the surface. Underneath, however, other emotions may be swirling around.

Once the abuse is over, it is not uncommon for children to struggle with anxiety, experience flashbacks or nightmares, resume bed-wetting, or begin to manifest unexplained physical symptoms. Often they think of themselves as worthless rather than precious. They may either become withdrawn or start to mimic some of the abusive behaviour they have seen, not realizing – unless someone explains it to them gently – that this is not a good way to be. Tantrums may erupt as the frustration of years of being made to keep secrets begins to be released. Older children may turn to self-harm, eating disorders, alcohol or drugs to numb the pain or bring some measure of control into their lives.

It's not unknown for a child to become angry with the parent who was abused rather than the abuser. Why wasn't she stronger? Why did he allow the abuse to persist? Children can become confused. After all, they will have heard the abuser's words and may need help teasing out the difference between truth and lies. With help, they can gradually begin to see how complex their home life was. Step by step, they can come to forgive all the adults whose actions have hurt or confused them.

It is worth seeking counselling for the young. That might be within the church, or it might be elsewhere, but they need to know they are loved, safe and valuable. They will need time and space to express the hard things they have experienced and seen – maybe through words, maybe through art or drama. They will need help to learn how adults are supposed to relate to one another in the home. Like their parents, they will benefit from grasping afresh the wonder of grace, and see legalism as something that brings only pain. Keeping lines of communication open between the children and the youth and children's workers at church is crucial. Children need to know they have somewhere to turn to process things in the light of Jesus' care – in that environment they can grow and thrive.

Should I encourage people to forgive?

Abusers love to talk about forgiveness. In Christian – or pseudo-Christian – homes forgiveness is often begged for, or demanded, after an incident of pain. It's used as a weapon that keeps people silent: 'You can't go and tell anyone about that – you've already said you've forgiven me. It's over and done with.'

That means, when the church speaks of forgiveness, it can often be assumed that what we mean is: pretend everything is OK, and allow yourself to be hurt again. But that is not what forgiveness involves!

Forgiveness is a process, not an event. It will take time, and cannot be forced. It is good though. As Christ has forgiven us when we don't deserve it, we are called to forgive others, even when they don't deserve it either.

The best time to speak of forgiveness is after true repentance is seen – once abusers have truly grasped the horrors of their actions, are sorry for the pain caused, and are genuinely committed to living differently for the glory of God. That's not always possible. Sometimes abusers never truly repent. They may be sorry they've been found out, but that's very different from wanting to change.

In either scenario, forgiveness is possible. We can encourage those who have been hurt to dwell afresh on the wonderful forgiveness they have received. Next, we can explain that forgiveness means releasing people from their debt to you, but it doesn't mean releasing them from the right (sometimes legal) consequences of their actions. It certainly doesn't mean automatic reconciliation, or permission for them to skip counselling or be trusted again, if they have refused to change.

After that, we can encourage people to ask God for the strength and the courage to forgive. We can help them imagine what life would be like for them without that unforgiveness in their heart. We can gently remind them that forgiveness is a mark of their faith. After all that, we can encourage them to say prayers of forgiveness. If it is safe to do so, they may even find it helpful to write a letter to their former abuser, expressing that forgiveness and their desire to see them flourish in the future (and if it's not safe, the letter can be written but not sent). This isn't a process to be rushed, but it is one that brings beauty and freedom into the lives of all involved.

The fallout may persist for weeks – it may persist for a decade or more – but, gradually, the grip of the past can loosen. Encouragement to persevere in walking closely with the Lord will bear fruit. Those who once had no hope can now overflow with confidence in the Lord. Those who have been trapped can come to know what it means to be wonderfully free.

I won't ever forget what he put me through. It's part of my story, and it always will be. But there is a bigger story at play – one that defines me to the core. That's the story of Jesus' work in my life, and that has a very happy ending.

Postscript

Do people ever truly overcome domestic abuse? There are thousands who do! I hear that truth from the lips of people I know every month – every year.

All will remember the pain from time to time. Some will struggle with the legacy until Jesus returns or calls them home. Many, however, in the hands of the living and loving God, will know true and lasting freedom. They will be able to enjoy a life abuse-free, rejoicing in the goodness of God and the mercies he brings every day.

Many will come to relish the new start that the end of abuse can bring. They will revel in new relationships, embrace new ways of living, realize long-dormant desires and go on to thrive as children of God. They will know the wonder of what Jesus promised in John 10:10: 'life . . . to the full'.

Some will go on to use their experiences within the local church or the wider community. Those who have overcome abuse are uniquely positioned to encourage those who are still in its grip. They embody the call of 2 Corinthians 1:3–5:

> Praise be to the God and Father of our Lord Jesus Christ, the Father of compassion and the God of all comfort, who comforts us in all our troubles, so that we can comfort those in any trouble with the comfort we ourselves receive from God. For just as we share abundantly in the sufferings of Christ, so also our comfort abounds through Christ.

Those of us who walk alongside will be changed by the process too. We will be struck more deeply by the depravity of sin, and have our hearts stirred to ever-greater compassion. We will see the goodness of God expressed in new and exciting ways, and know the privilege of being part of the process of true and lasting change. We'll be humbled by the faith and perseverance of those we walk alongside, and rejoice in the spiritual fruit that grows in them and us. Speaking personally, I have been humbled more times than I can recall.

Maybe most excitingly of all, we will know the wonder of God working in them and us, gradually bringing to completion the good work he has started (Philippians 1:6).

One day, we will know too the wonder of an abuse-free world; the new heavens and the new earth, free from suffering and death.

Freedom like that is well worth walking towards.

Appendix A:
Disclosure of abuse flow chart

Abuse is disclosed

⬇

Are there children involved?

⬇

No   Yes

Follow safeguarding guidelines
for children

⬇

Is there immediate risk to life?

⬇

No   Yes

Discuss options for involving
police/social services

⬇

Does the person want further help?

⬇

No   Yes

Offer to meet again   Call appropriate specialist
Write up notes   helpline to discuss options
Notify the church safeguarding   Arrange to meet again
officer   Notify the church safeguarding
                                          officer
                                          Write up notes

Appendix B:
Sample domestic abuse notice

This church:

- acknowledges, with sadness, that domestic abuse is a reality in this broken world;
- accepts that abuse can happen, both within the church and the wider community;
- understands that such pain can take the form of physical, sexual, psychological, financial, emotional or spiritual abuse. It can also include forced marriage and 'honour crimes';
- believes that such abuse is a serious transgression of God's law and the law of the land;
- undertakes to support and care for all those affected;
- commits itself to working in partnership with statutory agencies in order to bring an end to abuse;
- has a safeguarding officer who can offer advice in situations of abuse;

- encourages all those affected – either as perpetrators or those suffering – to contact the church, confident that seeking help is far better than staying silent;
- affirms that, in Christ, there is hope in every situation.

Church contact: [Name and contact details]

Local community contact: [Name and contact details]

Appendix C:
Prayers for the abused

Sometimes it can be hard for those who are being abused to pray. Giving them short prayers like the ones that follow can be a good first step towards encouraging people to run to the Lord with their own words.

> Why, LORD, do you stand far off?
>> Why do you hide yourself in times of trouble?
> (Psalm 10:1)

Lord, I don't understand what's going on in my life. I don't know what to do. I'm regularly hurt, frequently scared and sometimes I'm not sure you care. Please help me to see things as they truly are. Please help me to trust you more. Inspire my heart, Lord, so I have the strength to follow you into a future that is better than this.

But you, God, see the trouble of the afflicted;
　　you consider their grief and take it in hand.

The victims commit themselves to you;
　　you are the helper of the fatherless.
(Psalm 10:14)

Lord God, it's such a comfort to know that my struggles are not hidden from your sight. Thank you that you are so intimately involved in this world that you see all things. Thank you that you have promised to help and not leave life unchanged. Please help me to turn to you and my church family for the strength and direction I so desperately need.

Appendix D:
Useful resources and organizations

Books

Domestic abuse

Justin S. Holcomb and Lindsey A. Holcomb, *Is It My Fault?*
Hope and Healing for Those Suffering Domestic Violence
(Moody Press, 2014)

Jim Newheiser, *Help! Someone I Love Has Been Abused*
(Day One, 2010)

David Powlison, *Why Me? Comfort for the Victimized*
(Presbyterian & Reformed, 2003)

David Powlison, Paul David Tripp and Edward T. Welch,
Domestic Abuse: How to Help (Presbyterian & Reformed,
2002)

Edward T. Welch, *Living with an Angry Spouse: Help for Victims*
of Abuse (Presbyterian & Reformed, 2008)

Helping others change

Tim Chester, *You Can Change: God's Transforming Power for*
Our Sinful Behaviour and Negative Emotions (IVP, 2008)

Timothy S. Lane and Paul David Tripp, *How People Change* (New Growth Press, 2009)

David Powlison, *Speaking Truth in Love: Counsel in Community* (Evangelical Press, 2008)

Paul David Tripp, *Instruments in the Redeemer's Hands: People in Need of Change Helping People in Need of Change* (Presbyterian & Reformed, 2002)

Seeing God and ourselves as we truly are

Graham Beynon, *Emotions: Living Life in Colour* (IVP, 2012)

Graham Beynon, *Mirror, Mirror: Discover Your True Identity in Christ* (IVP, 2008)

Paul David Tripp, *Awe: Why It Matters for All We Think, Say and Do* (IVP, 2015)

Devotionals when suffering

Timothy Keller, *My Rock, My Refuge: A Year of Daily Devotions in the Psalms* (Hodder & Stoughton, 2015)

Kirsten Wetherell and Sarah Walton, *Hope When It Hurts* (The Good Book Company, 2017)

Marriage preparation

Christopher Ash, *Married for God: Making Your Marriage the Best It Can Be* (IVP, 2007)

Peter Jackson, *Preparing for Marriage: God's Plan for Your Life Together* (The Good Book Company, 2006)

John Piper, *This Momentary Marriage: A Parable of Permanence* (IVP, 2009)

Organizations

The organizations listed below all have specialist help to offer. Some may not be in line theologically with the content of this book, but their partnership on specific matters of housing, finance and law can be invaluable.

Biblical Counselling UK:
www.biblicalcounselling.org.uk

CCPAS (The Churches' Child Protection Advisory Service):
www.ccpas.co.uk

Dogs Trust:
https://www.moretodogstrust.org.uk/freedom-project/
freedom-project

National Domestic Violence Helpline:
www.nationaldomesticviolencehelpline.org.uk
(Tel: 0808 2000 247)

Refuge:
www.refuge.org.uk

Respect (for perpetrators of domestic violence):
www.respect.uk.net

Restored:
www.restoredrelationships.org

Victim Support:
https://www.victimsupport.org.uk

Notes

Introduction

1. <www.womensaid.org.uk>.
2. <www.refuge.org.uk>.
3. <https://www.gov.uk/guidance/domestic-violence-and-abuse>.
4. <www.refuge.org.uk>.
5. <www.eauk.org>.
6. <www.restoredrelationship.org>.

5 Stay or go?

1. DBS is the common acronym for the UK's Disclosure and Barring Service. This service assists organizations (including churches) to make safe decisions about who works and volunteers with more vulnerable groups by checking to see if an individual has been placed on a 'barred list'. Churches can access this service well through organizations such as the Churches' Child Protection Advisory Service (<https://www.ccpas.co.uk/>).

7 Speaking of a bigger God

1. Designed by Ninefootone Creative. Copyright © Helen Thorne.

8 Changing mirrors

1. Designed by Ninefootone Creative. Copyright © Helen Thorne.
2. 'If I Have Fled to Jesus'. Copyright © 2015 Michael Morrow. From the album *See Him Face to Face* (<www.co-mission.org/music/see-him-face-to-face>).

Biblical Counselling UK

Biblical Counselling UK seeks to serve Christ by fostering and supporting church members, pastors and teachers who are passionate about the transforming work of Christ that is accomplished through the personal ministry of the Word. We offer:

- conferences
- courses
- resources
- internships

For more information: www.biblicalcounselling.org.uk

**Christ-centred change, enabled by the Spirit,
through the ministry of the Word,
in the local church**

Biblical Counselling UK is registered as a Charitable Incorporated Organization in England and Wales, Registration No 1164965.